MAN

Existentialism of Jean Paul Sartre

Jean Paul Sartre
[1905-1980]

Existentialism of Jean Paul Sartre

DR. CHANDRA REKHA

MOTILAL BANARSIDASS PUBLISHERS
PRIVATE LIMITED • DELHI (INDIA)

Reprint : 2018
First Edition: Delhi, 2014

ISBN: 978-81-208-3703-4

MOTILAL BANARSIDASS
41 U.A., Bungalow Road, Jawahar Nagar, Delhi 110 007
1 B, Jyoti Studio Compound, Kennedy Bridge, Nana Chowk, Mumbai 400 007
203 Royapettah High Road, Mylapore, Chennai 600 004
236, 9th Main III Block, Jayanagar, Bengaluru 560 011
8 Camac Street, Kolkata 700 017
Ashok Rajpath, Patna 800 004
Chowk, Varanasi 221 001

Printed in India

by RP Jain at NAB Printing Unit,
A-44, Naraina Industrial Area, Phase I, New Delhi–110028
and published by JP Jain for Motilal Banarsidass Publishers (P) Ltd
41 U.A. Bungalow Road, Jawahar Nagar, Delhi-110007

I bow to the universal power which is
cause of our birth and death and
in between sustains us. I would like
to say thanks to my parents
[Mr. D.D. Soni and Mrs. Darshana Soni]
for their love and support.
I resolve to put in my truest
and deepest efforts in this work.

TABLE OF CONTENTS

Page No.

Chapter-2
The Human Reality

Chapter-4
Man as a Social Being

Chapter-5
Concluding Sartre's Concept of Man

Preface

For time immemorial man has been a mystery to the man. Many great minds have tried to find out the answers to all the questions pertaining to this mystery. Men tried it on the bases of scientific discoveries, natural phenomena or on the bases of their creative minds in the shape of religions, but everywhere we find that the key to the talisman does not lie in the outer world but in the inner depths of men. Discovery of this depth leads to one discipline known as philosophy. It is philosophy which rules every big or small effort as it evaluates every effort in the end and brings forth the results. Philosophy holds everything from the top. In short we can say that the philosophy is the beginning and the end of every kind of study and knowledge. Every person finds himself alone on this earth, despite of all the relations, friends, surroundings and crowd of the world. There is no door to enter inside the mind of other person. This enclosed world of man is called subjectivity of a man. Existentialism is such a philosophical discipline which sorts out the mystery of man on the bases of this subjectivity and on the bases of all the concepts which come out of it. It has been blamed on the existentialists that their writings bear the mark of personal experience but this fact has been misunderstood. The right point of view would be that they find their results from within, from a man, and they have universal application because even after a long duration of time, every person feels in these philosopher's work glimpses from their own secret subjectivity. This penetrating power of these philosophers's intelligence makes existentialism a widely read philosophy. The choice of Jean Paul Sartre for this book is influenced by the fact that his philosophy does not deal with a limited number of readers for typical philosophical topics but everyman will be benefitted as his philosophy presents a life style, strength of mind and open horizon of unlimited possibilities. Jean-Paul Sartre is a proponent of modern existentialism who explained his theory on atheistic bases. But it was not just a point of view; we meet in his works a great logical mind, widely read person and extraordinary intelligence. In short we can say we find in him a great writer of twentieth century.

Dr. Chandra Rekha

Introduction
[Existentialism]

Philosophy in general and existentialism in particular, is not just an academic study but also a mode of thought and action. Existentialism is an attitude and outlook that emphasizes human existence that is, the distinctive qualities of individual persons rather than men in abstract or nature and the world in general. Any person who leads his life with a subjective approach to every matter of life and believes in the freedom and capacity of man to choose, decide and influence his own as well as life of others by his decision is an existentialist. Faith in oneself is the main feature of an existentialist.

Existentialism is in favour of individual subjectivity, introspection and feeling. As it elaborates freedom of man to set course of his life with his choice and responsibility, it brings down the importance of determinism and encourage action in human life.

Rise of Existentialism is attributed to the destruction and human desolation attending the two world wars and the anxieties that stem from the continuing unrest in both world and domestic social failures but it is also an expression of the psychological and moral tensions that hold the individual in their grip in any age in any society.

At the opposite end from logical positivism with its emphasis on sensory empiricism, objectivity, logic and science; existentialism has been a reaction in favour of individualism, subjectivity, introspection and feeling. It is a philosophy not of things but of human situation. As against idealism it is an objection to the liberal doctrines of optimism and progress. As a champion of the concrete against the abstract, of life as opposed to logic, of the non-intellectual and irrational in contrast to intellectualism and of freedom as against mechanism anddeterminism. The roots of existentialism are very deep, taking us back to the days of Socrates, St. Paul, St. Augustine and Pascal. But in modern times it is grounded in the psychology of Kierkegaard, the philosophy of Nietzsche and the method and ontology of the phenomenologist Husserl. There is no single existentialist position. The philosophy varies with its proponents, but there is a common fund of doctrine that identifies them, nevertheless and indicates quite clearly their relation to the classical philosophic tradition. Their major and differentiating, thesis is the metaphysical pronouncement that "existence is prior to essence"; while in the established tradition "essence is prior to existence". It means for the existentialist, that human nature is determined by the course of life, rather than life by human nature.

In its theistic form, existentialism has been an important factor in the Neo-orthodox awakening that has marked theology since the First World War. Its emphasis on the negative qualities of man, on human estrangement and the tragedy of human existence, have supported the dogma of 'original sin' and the entire structure of eschatological, theology, secular or more often called, atheistic. Existentialism has been popularized especially since the Second World War by numerous expressions in fiction, drama and poetry, particularly by its French partisans under the leadership of Jean Paul Sartre. In its technical formulations, recent existentialism is largely a German product, its foremost representatives being Paul Tillich, Karl Jaspers and Martin Heidegger. Existentialism is not a school of thought but a branch of philosophy. In different times when different tried to free themselves from established dogmas, rituals, rules and tried to assert freedom of man to accept or reject anything, existentialism was born, it does not have set rules, as it is a way to look at something according to individual approach.

Existentialism is the way we act, the way we believe and the way we want ourselves to be. In the life of an existentialist every moment is having existential quality as he does not have to prove anything theoretically but choosing in a right manner, in a whole heartedly manner right course of action. It does not mean that existentialism discards everything, which is in fashion, but it always chooses the right, which saves his inwardness and subjectivity. Common Features among Different Existentialists are as follows:

1. The commonest fact among the various existentialist philosophies of the present is the fact that they all arrive from a so-called existentialist experience, which assumes a different form in each of them. It is found in Jaspers, for instance, in awareness of bitterness of being, by Heidegger through experiencing propulsion towards death and by Sartre in a general nausea. The existentialists do not conceal the fact that their philosophy originate in such experience. That is why existentialist philosophy always bears the stamp of personal experience, even in Heideggar.
2. The The existentialist takes so-called existence, as the supreme objective of enquiry, but the meaning, which they attach to the word, is extremely difficult to determine. However in each case it signifies a peculiarly human mode of being. 'Man' is a term which is used and is generally replaced by 'there-ness (Dasien)', 'existence', 'ego' 'being for oneself'; is unique in possessing existence, more precisely, man does not possess but he is his existence, if man has an essence, either this essence is his existence or it is the consequence of it.
3. Existence is conceived as absolutely acculturistic, it never is but freely creates itself, it becomes, it is a

projection, with each instant, it is more or less than it is. The existentialists often support this by the statement that existence is the same as temporality.

4. The difference between actualism and that of life philosophy is accounted for by the existentialist regarding man as pure subjectivity and not as manifestation of a broader life process. Subjectivity is understood in a creative sense; man creates himself freely and is his freedom.
5. Yet it would be thoroughly misguided to conclude from this that the existentialists regard man as shut up within himself. On the contrary, man is an incomplete and open reality, thus his nature pins him down tightly and necessarily to the world and to other men in particular. This double dependence is assumed by all representatives of existentialism, and in such a way that human existence seem to be inserted in the world, so that man at all times not only faces a determinate situation but is, his situation. On the other hand, they assume that there is a special connection between men, which like the situation, gives existence its peculiar quality. This is the meaning of Heidegger's 'togetherness', Jasper's 'communication' and Marcel's 'thou'.
6. All existentialist repudiate the distinction between subject and object, thereby discounting the value of intellectual knowledge for philosophical purposes. According to them, true knowledge is not achieved by understanding but through experiencing reality, this experience is primarily caused by the dread with which man becomes aware of his finitude and the frailty in that position of being thrust into the world and condemned to death (Heidegger).

Several other common features of minor importance may be discerned in existentialism, but deep differences between its individual representatives are equally evident. For example, Marcel is like Kierkegaard in being a theist whereas Jaspers adopts a sort of transcendence which should not be interpreted as theism, pantheism, or atheism, because Jaspers repudiates all of these. Heaideggear's philosophy at first seems to be atheist but his unexpanded statements definitely exclude the interpretation finally; Sartre tries to work out a professed and logical atheism.

The aim and method of individual existentialist philosophers are equally different, Heidegger tries to establish ontology in the Aristotelian sense, and his use of a strict method is copied by Sartre, Jaspers refuses to admit any sort of ontology as a mean of elucidating existence but expands a metaphysical system, and the method which he employs, seems to be a very flexible one. On the basis of their belief in God or any transcendental reality existentialism is divided into two parts:

1. Theistic Existentialism: Leading names related to this stream are:
   Soren Kierkegaard, Gabriel Marcel, Karl Jaspers
2. Atheistic Existentialism: Leading names related to this stream are:
   Albert Camus, Martin Heidegger, Jean Paul Sartre

All other classical philosophies give objective knowledge about world and God, and leave man at very subordinate position. Now existentialism holds the rein where man is said to possess no individuality in this world, according to the theories based on abstract principles.

Philosophies are not physical entities having their own existences but they are wise creations of human mind so it is man who thinks, feels and creates. Then how can a man negate his own existence in the favor of objective realities. Existentialism grants man a supreme position. With or without God man is an important creature. Man takes birth, crates his own essence by choosing the life style and being a particular kind of person and then dies as a particular person. So throughout our life we are particulars.

All these things make us feel that maximum times we have personal moments in life and we cannot be described in terms of biological entity only. Maximum philosophies try to discover the truth in the form of theories which describe man and world as facts. Man seen as a small cog fitted in the whole machine to make it run, but actually situation is different. When I get my hand cut, only I have to bear the pain; if something fatal comes my way to achieve something, I feel depression and nobody can take away failure from me. Some things in life cannot be changed; birthplace, family of birth, physical incapability, physical surroundings, beauty, health etc. Because of unfavourable circumstances a more capable man is left behind than the less capable man having more favourable circumstances.

Every failure and trouble is not always psychological, a lot of times it is real existence, which cannot be ignored by optimistic approach only. People who criticized existentialism by calling it philosophy of crisis, Nihilism, Pessimism etc. do not understand its essence.

It is a rise from problems, understanding them fully and then getting a way of life which is action oriented and finally extremely optimistic. As every person has a different life from the life of others, experiences vary from person to person and so is the approach. It is the reason why all existentialist philosophers cannot be explained by a single theory.

Jean-Paul Sartre was a French philosopher of twentieth century and his theory is unique of its kind because he proved logically and ontologically that man is absolutely free and a God for himself. Although he borrowed a lot from Kierkegaard and Heidegger but his philosophical method is unique of its kind. Sartre ventured to affirm that 'existence precedes essence' to the finest detail and made this dictum a hallmark of existentialism.

In the modern times anybody who talks about existentialism, associates it with the name of Sartre, as he was the one who explained the man with complete importance and freedom, even against God. For Sartre the subjective is real, and truth is subjectivity, man making himself the being he is, is what Sartre means by subjectivity. This assertion continues part of his principle of existentialism. His man owes complete responsibility for his actions and its Consequences, throughout life standing alone in the world Sartre's man is the strongest individual.

Jean Paul Sartre also published his existentialist thoughts in the form of literature, poetry and drama. Sartre was the most impressive of all existentialists to influence others. His work area was limited, concerned with action, will and responsibility. Main turning point in his philosophy was wartime when he himself was kept as a war prisoner. Due to his experiences he felt it as a blow to human subjectivity. Then he decided to establish subjective approach of man in a firm manner. He was impressed by the method of Rene Descartes (1596-1650) and the Phenomenology of Edmund Gustav Albert Husserl(1859-1938). We can see that all existentialist philosophers wanted to assert subjectivity of man with different feelings and different styles but ultimately we will find implication of all kinds of philosophies in the domain of humanity.

Every age in the world had different problems and so were the solutions. We are living in an age which is a kind of saturation in all the fields for example science, technology, religion. Life is becoming more and more complex and we are living amidst crime, corruption and war. Everyday seems to be the doom's day. Globalization has made the world geographically smaller so It is the strongest need of time to feel individuality. Although a lot of people understand it but ignore freedom of others in an aggressive way. That in turn is resulting, in less individual freedom. So existentialism: with a right approach to humanity where individual is concerned with individual for a better bonding and better world, is a great help.

The aim of this book is to explain Jean Paul Sartre's simple and pure thought of freedom and humanity combined together. It's a great insight into inner depths of man. Whether someone believes in God or not is a different question to be sorted out by the individual concerned but it only should be agreeable with existential freedom and humanity. What is important is the existential fact that when man understands other man, he enters a world of own values, feelings and passions. This is a remarkable fact in the light of which Sartre's existentialism may be understood.

Introduction to the Philosophy of Jean Paul Sartre

Jean-Paul Sartre is one of the best known philosophers of the 20th Century. He was an existentialist philosopher; Sartre was a leading figure of existential movement in France. The central theme of his philosophy is atheistic and goes with the dictum that "Existence precedes Essence". He explains that in man and man alone, existence precedes essence.

> *This simply means that man first is and only subsequently is that or this. In a word man must create his own essence. It is throwing himself into the world, suffering there, struggling there, that he gradually defines himself. And the definition always remains open ended. We cannot say what this man is, before he dies or what mankind is, before it has disappeared.*[1]

Sartre used different terms as mankind, human-reality, human being and for-itself (pour-soi) with the same meaning. Sartre developed existentialism as a philosophical position in *Being and Nothingness [L'Extre et le Neant]*, published in 1943. The basic ontological premise of Sartre's existentialism is negative and atheistic. He explains that, "Existentialism is nothing but an attempt to draw all the consequences from a consistent atheistic position". Atheistic existentialism states that:

> *If God does not exist there is at least one being in whom existence precedes essence, a being that exists before he can be defined by any concept, and this being is man.*[2]

Although Sartre received his doctorate in philosophy in 1929 from the Ecole Normale Superieur, his philosophical journey had started in the childhood, which is obvious from the autobiography, of Sartre which is known as:

The words, the Autobiography of Jean Paul Sartre.[3]

It was written when he was 59 years old, but it describes only his first ten years of age. It is considered as a masterpiece of self-analysis of a child. At the age of nine he started writing stories for children that explained his truthfulness, innocence, an effort to understand human relations, self-respect, values and his philosophical bent of mind.

The strategy of 'indirect communication' has been an instrument of existential philosophers, which serves as a kind of suggestion and not a lecture. Plays and novels written by Sartre were successful to spread existential thoughts. We can call him a philosophical litterateur. His philosophy is influenced by Edmund Gustav Albert Husserl [1859-1938] and Martin Heidegger [1889-1976]. Sartre read the leading phenomenologist of the day, Husserl and Heidegger, at the French institute of Berlin in [1933-34]. Adopting and adapting the methods of phenomenology, Sartre sets out to develop an ontological account of what it is to be a human. In his philosophy he somewhere mentions about Kant, Leibniz and Berkley also but basic concepts are influenced from phenomenology, sometimes in favour and sometimes against it.

He prized Husserl's restatement of the 'principle of Intentionality' [all consciousness aims at or 'intends' an other-than-consciousness], that seems to free the thinker from the inside-outside epistemology inherited from Rene Descartes [1596-1650], while retaining the immediacy and certainty that Cartesians prized so highly. Sartre published an essay entitled 'Husserl's central idea". In this essay, Sartre rejects the epistemology of Descartes and Neo-Kantians and their view of consciousness' relationship to the world. Consciousness is not related to the world by virtue of a set of mental representations and acts of mental synthesis that combine such representations to provide us with our knowledge of the external world. Husserl's intentional theory of consciousness provides the only acceptable alternative. Consciousness and the world are immediately given together: the world essentially external to consciousness is essentially related to it. The only appropriate image for intentionality and our knowing relationship to the world is that of an 'explosion'. 'To know is to 'explode toward' an object in the world, an object beyond oneself, over there, towards that which is not one, out of oneself. This principle of Intentionality is exploited in Sartre's ontology by saying that Human Reality [Heidegger's Dasien] is in the world primarily via its practical concerns and not its epistemic relationships.

As far as Heidegger is concerned, we find philosophy of Sartre very close to that of Heidegger's. Heidegger's concepts of Dasein, Nothingness, Possibility, Temporality, Death etc., are all taken as a base by Sartre to explain his own philosophy which he calls Phenomenological Ontology. The Philosophy which was explained in *Sein and Zeit* of Heidegger is developed and clarified in 'Being and Nothingness' of Sartre. Style of Heidegger is mystical and complex, but that of Sartre is simple and logical. Like Husserl and Heidegger, Sartre distinguished ontology from metaphysics and favoured the former. In his case, ontology is primarily descriptive and classificatory concerned with 'how and what' whereas, metaphysics purports to be causally explanatory concerned with 'why' offering accounts about the ultimate origins and ends of individuals and of the universe as a whole. Point of view of Sartre about metaphysics is that it raises questions we cannot answer.

Sartre's Being and Nothingness is the culmination of his philosophical thoughts, as far as his previous works are concerned and serves as a clue or base for his later works, whether philosophical or literary. Its descriptive method moves from the most abstract to the highly concrete. Sartre's methodology is Husserlian insofar as it is a form of intentional and eidetic, as 'about' something. It means that the acts by which consciousness assigns meaning to objects is under analysis, and that, what is sought in the particular mark on this view by presenting the consciousness as being transparent, i.e. having no inside' but rather as being a 'fleeing' towards the world.

He differs from Husserl's Methodology on the point that, Husserl claims his methods as uncovering the essence of things but Sartre shows no interest in this, Husserl eidetic analysis bring out the essence that is hidden in 'fluid unclarity' (Husserl, Ideas,1) but for Sartre it does not deliver something fixed immanent to the phenomenon. Sartre's methodology still claims to uncover that which is essential, but thereby recognizes that phenomenal experience is essentially fluid.

In *Being and Nothingness* Sartre begins by analysis of the 'Being'. It consists of two distinct and irreducible categories the In-itself [en-soi] and the For-itself [pour-soi]. In-itself means non-conscious objects, while for-itself is the conscious being, the man. The man is subject of study for Sartre, as everything remaining moves around him. The man as consciousness is the being by whom nothingness comes into the world. It means that man himself is Being and Nothingness. Anguish is born in this nothingness, which in turn gives way to two kinds of behaviour. If man flees it, he stops being caught in Bad-faith and if he makes choices, calculating possibilities for his future, it means exercising a freedom. This freedom to choose a projected future is the aim and salvation of man as the choices which a man makes out of freedom give value to the life. Choices which are made throughout life are related to the fundamental choice, which is choosing a kind of being. All acts whether professional, emotional or else add value to it, ultimately giving a value of life. Atheism of Sartre becomes prominent by giving utmost importance to human freedom against determinism. On the other hand to land in Bad-faith is to give way to determinism sometimes so to deny that attitude calling Bad-faith is to deny God in disguise. Few dictums are quoted by Sartre directly denying existence of God also. Sartre describes a method in the name of "existential psychoanalysis" that interprets our actions to uncover the fundamental project that unifies our lives. To understand the ontology of *Being and Nothingness* it is necessary to understand that when and how these ideas originated.

In an article called *La Transcendance de L'Ego Esguisse D'une Description Phenomenologique [Transcendence of the Ego: An Existentialist Theory of Consciousness]-1936,* Sartre while keeping within the general province of phenomenology challenged Husserl's concept of the *'Transcendental Ego'*. He agreed with Husserl that consciousness is about objects or, as they say, it 'intends' at them rather than forming within itself a duplicate, an inner representation of an outward object. Sartre says that material object of consciousness (or. 'objects of intension) exist in their own right, independent and without any residue accumulating in them from our awareness of them.

The new theme of the essay where Sartre differed from Husserl was that the person's ego itself is also 'in the world', an object of consciousness to be discovered, rather than the totally known subject of consciousness. One more important thing of the essay is Sartre's rejection of the primacy of the Cartesian cogito. In the Descartes' formula 'I think therefore I am' – the consciousness which says 'I am' is not actually the consciousness which thinks instead it is secondary activity. Descartes has confused spontaneous doubt, which is a consciousness, with methodological doubt, which is an act. Cartesian cogito is not one with the doubting consciousness but has reflected upon it. In other words this cogito is not Descartes' doubting, it is Descartes' reflecting upon the doubting. "I doubt, therefore I am" is really "I am aware that I doubt, therefore I am." The Cartesian cogito is reflective and its object is not itself but the original consciousness of doubting. The consciousness which doubted is now reflected on by the cogito but was never itself reflective; its only object is the object which it is conscious of as doubtful. Through these arguments Sartre establishes that pre-reflective cogito is the primary consciousness.

Thus the very nature of consciousness is such that for it to be and to know itself are one and the same thing. Sartre finally draws out two types of consciousness. As consciousness of an object is consciousness of being conscious of an object, so by nature all consciousness is self-consciousness. But deliberate thinking about consciousness is a new act and posits self-awareness as an object of reflection. The pre-reflective consciousness is called non-positional self-consciousness and non-thetic self-consciousness. The positional and thetic self-consciousness is conscious de soi in which consciousness deliberately reflects upon its own acts and states and in so far is possible posits itself as an object. The Cartesian cogito, belongs to the second order. In the article, Sartre lays down two fundamental principles concerning the pre-reflective consciousness.

1. He follows Husserl in holding that all consciousness is consciousness of something that is intentional and directive, pointing to a transcendent object other than itself. It served as a foundation for 'Being-in-itself' and Man's 'Being-in-the-world' in the Being and Nothingness.

2. The pre-reflective cogito is non-personal. We cannot say in the beginning that "I am conscious of the chair", but that "there is consciousness of the chair". The Ego (including both 'I' and 'Me') come into existence only when the original consciousness has been made the object of reflection. Thus there is never any Ego-consciousness but only consciousness of the Ego.

So according to Sartre, the Ego is not in the consciousness, which is utterly translucent, Ego is in the world and like the world it is object of the consciousness. It does not mean that Ego is material but it is not a subject that manipulates or directs consciousness. We should not say 'my consciousness' but rather 'consciousness of me'.

Consciousness is particular because it is conscious of particular object and not the whole universe. Thus the consciousness of two persons are always individual and always self-consciousness. But to be individual and to be self-conscious does not mean to be personal.

Ego is on the side of the psychic. Sartre makes a distinction between consciousness in its purity and psychic qualities. Psychic qualities are ordinarily thought of as the personality. My immediate reaction of repulsion or attraction to someone is a consciousness. The unity which the reflective consciousness establishes between this reaction and earlier similar ones establishes my state of love and hate. My Ego stands as the ideal unity of all of my states, qualities and actions, but as such it is an object pole and not a subject. It is the flux of consciousness constituting itself as the unity of itself.

> *Thus the Ego is a 'synthesis' of interiority and transcendence.*[4]

The Ego stands in the same relation to all the psychic objects of consciousness, as the unity called 'the world' stands in the relation to the physical objects of consciousness. Both 'Ego' and 'world' are transcendent objects-in reality, ideal unities. The difference is that psychic is dependent on consciousness and in one sense has been constituted by it where as objects in the world are not created by consciousness. 'I' and the 'Me' these are but two aspects of the Ego. Although Ego serves to unify consciousness but consciousness infinitely overflows the 'I' which ordinarily serves to unify it, the foundation of his view of anguish, the germ of his doctrine of 'Bad faith' and a basis for his belief in the absolute freedom of consciousness.

> *Consciousness is afraid of its own spontaneity because it feels itself to be beyond freedom.*[5]

Vertigo or anguish is results of realizing this infinite freedom. There is nothing to prevent consciousness from making a wholly new choice of its way of being. Ego becomes a mean of consciousness to protect itself from limitless freedom, the freedom which can threaten the bonds of personality. Here is the origin of Bad-faith, when consciousness practices the possibility of wavering back and forth that is consciousness demanding the privileges of freedom, yet seeking refuge from the responsibilities of freedom, by pretending to be concealed and confined in an already established ego.

Nausea (La Nause'e)-1938, a novel written by Sartre is the richest in philosophical content. Existentialism is concerned with concrete emotions of happiness, unhappiness, anguish, despair, ethical problems, purposes and conducts of man. Through the novel Sartre is exploring the world, facing all the problems and trying to find meaning of Existence, his own existence and that of the things. This novel deals with everything on concrete level. He explains that to live alone without social life means to be alone it is not to exist in a true sense. One has to join with others in order to give importance to what you feel or what you are doing. Life of a lonely person becomes purposeless. In utter disappointment he writes:

> *When you live alone, you even forget what it is to tell a story. Plausibility disappears at the same time as friends, It is unusual for a man on his own to feel like laughing.*[6]

In *The Transcendence of the Ego* the objects which were intended by consciousness, get their full meaning and explanation in this novel. These objects are termed as in-itself in the *Being and Nothingness*. Their contingency and facticity touch to the consciousness to such an extent that it results in nausea which means a feeling of a sweet disgust, an unbearable contingency, after perceiving and touching them.

> *Objects ought not to touch, since they are not alive. You use them, you put them back in place, you live among them: they are useful nothing more. But they touch me, it's unbearable. I am afraid of entering in contact with them, just as if they were living animals.*[7]

Idea of temporality is presented in the Nausea in the form of three temporal ecstasies past, present and future. Present and future are so much combined that when future reaches we find that it was already there. As far as past is concerned, it is related to present. Memories at present maintain our past. Thus without past, no present and no future can be maintained.

> *I build my memories with my present. I am rejected, abandoned in the present. I try in vain to rejoin the past: I cannot escape from myself.*[8]

This idea of temporality finds its fullness in *Being and Nothingness*. But here Sartre just wants to describe that past never returns. We never notice when future becomes present and present becomes past. This irreversibility of time is the greatest adventure of life. Man is searching for the meaning of life. The writer decides that loneliness, society, feeling of adventure, temporality, there is nothing which can describe meaning of life. It is the man himself, who must choose to give meaning to life.

> *I cannot imagine what is required of me. Yet I must choose.*[9]

The important thing is that even in meaningless life when man says that "I am myself", it gives value to his existence. Because whatever he questions and before he decides to choose he calls it an adventure that it is I who is doing all this. Further Sartre criticizes prevalent meaning of life when he goes to a museum where portraits of famous and successful people are there and the famous formula of people about success is that all of them gave meaning to life by getting married, earning money and fame. They were entitled to everything: to life, to work, to wealth, to authority, to respect and finally to immortality. But Sartre does not call it authentic existence, as he says that life of a person without purpose can be compared to a stone, a microbe, a plant. In this kind of life man feels a depression.

> *My existence was beginning to cause me serious concern. Was I a mere fragment of imagination?*[10]

This way trying to find meaning of existence he has the realization that being in general and he himself in particular are de trop. Existence itself is contingent, gratuitous and unjustifiable. It is absurd as there is no reason for it, no purpose to give it meaning and no direction. There is nothing outside it, Being is just there. Things overflow all the relations and designations which he can attach to them, he himself being an existent cannot escape this original contingency, this superfluity.

> *We were a heap of existents, irritated, embarrassed at ourselves, we hadn't the slightest reason to be there, none of us, each one, confused, vaguely*

> *alarmed, felt de trop in relation to the others. De trop : it was the only relationship I could establish between these trees, these gates, these stones and I: soft, weak, obscene, digesting, juggling with dismal thoughts – I, too was de trop.* [11]

The following passage from the Being and Nothingness conveys same feelings:

> *Being-in-itself is neither possible nor impossible. It is. This is what consciousness expresses in anthropomorphic terms by saying that being is superfluous (de trop) – uncreated, without reasor for being, without any connection with another being, being-in-itself is de trop for eternity.* [12]

In search of authentic existence when man comes across facticity, consciousness and body he feels a certain kind of restlessness and anguish. This is nausea. Nausea appears when man feels the in-itself, or when he finds meaninglessness of life, or when he feels cruelty of temporality and ultimately when all the existents, the trees, stones, objects, air etc. reveal their solid existence, more solid than that of man's existence. He comes to know that world changes but every time he finds in his consciousness change related to the world, he feels that he himself applies meaning to the world.

> *It was a sort of sweet disgust. How unpleasant it was. And it came from the pebble; I'm sure that, it passed from the pebble into my hands. Yes that's it. That's exactly it: a sort of Nausea in the hands.*[13]

This thing becomes more obvious in his further creation the Emotion where he explains that emotion is capable to change meanings and relations of the world.Man is surrounded by strong objects which are called in-itself from all around. It is impossible to escape them. They pounce on their existence upon men from all direction. It fills man with the feeling of nausea.

> *The Nausea is not inside me: I can feel it over there, on the wall, on the braces, everywhere around me. It is one with the cafe; it is I who am inside it.*[14]

Nausea reveals the body to consciousness, when facts and anguish surround us and we get disturbed, our body in terms of rebellion is revealed to us. Here nausea establishes a relation between in-itself, for-itself and facticity.

> *The thing which was waiting has sounded the alarm, it has pounced upon me, it is slipping into me, I am full of it. It's nothing: I am the thing. Existence, liberated, released, surges over me. I exist. I exist It's sweet, so sweet, so slow and light. I move, gently, gently. There is some frothy water in my mouth – this pool is me too. And the tongue and the throat is me.*[15]

Being and Nothingness systematized the anguished paradoxes and ironies of Nausea. In it Sartre argues that the self must be understood in relation to the world of things. The self is for-itself and things are in-itself.

In the *Psychology of Imagination* – a treatise on phenomenological psychology (1940), we find the basis for Sartre's later presentation of 'Nothingness'. In this we find a difference between imagination and perception.

In the imagination the object is either as absent, as non-existent, or as existing Elsewhere, or as neutralized (i.e. not posited as existing). In this positing conscious-ness exercises its peculiar power of nihilation. If an object is to be posited as absent or not existing, then there must be involved the ability to constitute an emptiness or nothingness with respect to it. In connection to imagination and nothingness, Sartre introduces two terms

– 'being-in-the-world' and 'being-in-the-midst-of-the-world'. Being-in-the-midst-of-the-world is to be one with the world as in the case of objects. Consciousness is in-the-world. It means that consciousness is not one with but involved in the world, maintaining the separation between consciousness and things in the world. Consciousness is consciousness of objects; it means it is not the object. In short, there is a power of withdrawal in consciousness such that it can nihilate (encase with a region of non-being) the objects of which it is conscious.

Imagination requires two of these nihilating acts. The first one is Imaginative act, that is constituting, isolating and nihilating. It constitutes the world as a world, as before consciousness there was no world but only full, undifferentiated being. It then nihilates the world from the particular point of view. And then by a second act of nihilation, it isolates the objects from the world as out-of-reach.

The conditions of possibility for an imagining consciousness are the same as for consciousness in general. If consciousness could not imagine, this could only be because it lacked the power of negating withdrawl which Sartre calls nihilation; and this would result in so submerging consciousness in the world that it could no longer distinguish itself from the world. In the book Sartre also links the ideas of Nothingness and Freedom. In order to imagine, the consciousness must be free from all specific reality and this freedom must be able to define itself by a 'being-in-the-world' which is at once the constitution and negation of the world. This means that consciousness must be able to affect the emergence of the 'unreal'.

> *The unreal is produced outside of the world by a consciousness which stays in the world, and it is because he is transcendently free that man can imagine.*[16]

In the *Emotions (1939)* – In this Sartre discusses consciousness and organization of the world from a different point of view. According to Sartre emotion is simply a way by which consciousness chooses to live its relationship to the world. On what we might call the everyday pragmatic level of existence, our perception constitutes the world in terms of demands.

> *The world of our desires, our needs and our acts appears if it were furrowed with strict and narrow paths which lead to one or the other determined end, that is, to the appearance of a created object.*[17]

All of this is an anticipation of the hierarchy of 'instrumental complexes' which is explained in Being and Nothingness. These instrumental complexes give way to rise of emotions when we chose to ignore or neglect them. So it can be said that according to Sartre rise of emotions is on the ground of negative feelings.

He explains that, this world with its hodological marking is difficult, if my plans meet with utter frustration, I may seek to transform the whole character of the world which blocks me. As to change the whole world is not possible I make a magical transformation, and this is to make new ways and relationships through a change in myself.

So Sartre concludes by saying that emotion is a consciousness' personal relation to the world and as such can be temporarily satisfying, but it is fundamentally ineffective and transient with no direct power to affect the environment.

Sartre major philosophical text *The Critique of Dialectical Reason* appeared in 1960 and an essay that came to served as its introduction *Search for a Method* appeared in 1957. In it Hegelian and Marxist presence became prominent. In it Sartre combines Hegelian-Marxist dialectic with an existentialist 'psychoanalysis' that incorporates individual responsibility into class relationships, adds a properly existentialist dimension of moral responsibility to a Marxist emphasis on collective and structural causality.

Consciousness and the in-itself in his earlier work are assumed by praxis (human activity in its material context) and the practico-inert respectively in the *critique of Dialectical Reason*. Praxis is dialectical in the Hegelian sense that it surpasses and subsumes its other, the practico-inert. The latter, like the in-itself is inert but as 'practico' is the sedimentation of previous praxis. Thus speech act would be examples of praxis but language would be practico-inert: social institutions are practico-inert but the actions they both foster and limit are praxis.

Sartre accords an ontological primacy to individual praxis while recognizing its enrichment as group member of a praxis that sustains predicates such as command / obedience and right / duty that properly is its own. The concepts of praxis, practico-inert and mediating third form the basis of a social ontology. Here mediating third denotes the group member as such and fields a collective subject without reducing the respective agents to mere ciphers of some collective consciousness.

Having understood all the major themes in Sartre's philosophy we can analyze the main ontological study of man Being and Nothingness. It is logical, based on concrete study that's why it is called phenomenological ontology. It is in connection with the study of facticity, that he presents the most detailed analysis of the problem of freedom. Sartre provides his for-itself with absolute freedom.

Chapter-1
Man as Being and Nothingness

Being and Nothingness

Sartre's theory of reality includes explanation of being and nothingness. This being is to be understood with reference to the nothingness as being is not complete without it. Sartre says that 'Is' can be understood because there is, 'is not', in this way both being and nothingness are complimentary concepts of the real. Study and detailed structural description of being that includes both conscious and non-conscious, helps to bring out the concept of man, the man who is centre of the universe and maker of himself. This man creates his own being carrying a nothingness within himself and assimilates nonliving factor of reality in his life. This whole process is the theory; Jean Paul Sartre is basically concerned with.

Being

The study of Being is based on two prevalent methods being, 'Metaphysics' and 'Ontology'. Ontology is considered a part of metaphysics. Ontology being logical construction and based on real life instances, Sartre chooses ontology, for he finds it possible for man, as metaphysics being beyond the capability of man. Sartre describes structural analysis of Being, making a start with theories concerned with exterior and interior of Being.

Sartre rejects the theories that explain that exterior is a superficial covering or appearance hiding the true nature or reality of a thing, the reality which can be intuitioned or guessed but can never be reached being interior, or some accepting the exterior the only reality. He mentions about phenomenology of Husserl and Heidegger, and duality of phenomenon and noumenon in the theory of Kant. Husserl believed that through eidetic reduction we can reach to the essence of consciousness beyond the concrete phenomena. As far as objects are concerned, their appearance manifests directly their structural object form. Husserl compares it to the mathematical form, where concrete shapes are based on ideas of square; triangle etc. or we can say that concrete shapes give ideas about ideal shapes. It resembles to the Plato's theory of ideas. In both cases, there is a little difference in appearance and reality. Although the difference is not much obvious as in that of Heidegger's theory and that of Kant's.

Sartre rejects it calling dualism but accepts it partially. As far as consciousness is concerned, he accepts Husserl's theory of intentionality. About phenomena Sartre agreed that object of knowledge was simply what was given or presented to human consciousness; it had nothing to do with any noumenal object at all.

A profound difference in appearance and reality is obvious in the theories of Kant and Heidegger. According to Kant whatever appears and is object of human knowledge is phenomenon, and the thing-in-itself which hides behind this phenomena and can never be known by human reality through direct experience is called noumenon. This noumenon is underlying reality of the concrete world; assumed as soul and God.

Heidegger's idea is somewhat similar to that of Kant's idea. For Heidegger human reality is 'ontic-ontological'. Here ontic means concrete relations in the midst of the world while ontological means structural study of beings to reach to the hidden reality that is Being. Here we find a distinction between beings (concrete world's objects and human beings) and Being

(Basic underlying reality). Heidegger suggests that through the ontic that is relatively related beings of the world, an ontological study can help us to reach to the 'Being'.

Sartre accepts the ontic of Heidegger but does not accept the idea of underlying reality. For Sartre, the being of existent is exactly what it appears. What it is, is absolute, for it reveals itself as it is. He says that:

> *The genius of Proust is neither the work considered in isolation nor the subjective ability to produce it; it is the work considered as the totality of the manifestations of the person.*[18]

Sartre gets rids of dualism of appearance and reality simplifying the theme on the basis of practical observation of concrete realities and logical construction out of them. He explains that exterior and interior of any existent are not opposed. In an existent, the appearance which manifests it cannot be defined as exterior or interior but they are in totality, the thing itself. The appearances refer to the total series of appearances and not to a hidden reality which would drain to itself all the being of the existent. And the appearance for its part is not an inconsistent manifestation of this being.

If we no longer believe in the being behind-the-appearance, then appearance becomes full positivity. Its essence is an appearing which is no longer opposed to being but on the contrary is the measure of it. Sartre states like this:

> *The appearance does not hide the essence, it reveals it. It is the essence. The essence of an existent is no longer a property sunk in the cavity of this existent; it is the manifest law which presides over the succession of its appearances, it is the principle of the series.*[19]

All the appearances of an existent are well connected in

a series to provide a full meaning to it. So observation of concatenations of appearances proves that Being is a phenomenal being, that is structural reality or manifestation of essence of existence.

The first consequence of the theory of the phenomenon is that the appearances do not refer to being as Kant's phenomenon refers to the noumenon. Since there is nothing behind the appearance, and it indicates only itself and the total series of appearances, it cannot be supported by any being other than its own. The appearance cannot be the thin film of nothingness which separates the being-of-the-subject from the absolute-being. Thus the phenomenon which is manifested to all is explained by Sartre as follows.

The Phenomenon

The phenomenon is what manifests itself. Being manifests itself to all in some way, since we can speak of it and since we have a certain comprehension of it. Thus there must be for it a phenomenon of being, an appearance of being, capable of description as such. Sartre says that Being will be disclosed to us by some kind of immediate access, boredom, nausea etc. in us and the description of the phenomenon of being as it manifests itself will be on the bases of ontology, thus ontological interpretation is going to serve as an intermediary.

The world manifests itself through different phenomena; living and non-living. All these phenomena taken by the appearance indicate towards the Being thus the world on the whole is the Being.

> *The existent is a phenomenon; this means that it designates as an organized totality of qualities. It designates itself and not its being. Being is simply the condition of all revelation. It is being-for-*

> *revealing (etre-pour-devoiler) and not revealed being (etre devoite).*[20]

What determines the being of the appearance is the fact that it appears. And since we have restricted reality to the phenomenon, we can say of the phenomenon that reality is as it appears. The same thing is explained in the novel Nausea. According to Sartre the feeling of nausea in a man is the revelation of Being in concrete terms. The whole world, including the man and the objects is termed as Being. Sartre defines nausea by saying that the nausea is recognition of my body to me, my consciousness to me the other world to me. Thus nausea reveals body, consciousness and the world through certain phenomenal appearances. This philosophic concept of nausea reveals the concrete existence of man in the midst of the world.

> *The thing which was waiting has sounded the alarm, it has pounced upon me, it is slipping into me, I am full of it. It's nothing: I am the thing. Existence, liberated, released, surges over me. I exist. I exist. It's sweet, so sweet, so slow and light. You'd swear that it flows in the air all by itself. It moves. Little brushing movements everywhere, which melt and disappear. Gently, gently. There is some frothy water in my mouth. This pool is me too. And the tongue and the throat is me. I see my hand spread out on the table. It's alive – It's me.*[21]

This nausea in terms of existence has been explained by Sartre saying that this exixtence is there, around us, in us, it is us.

> *Did I dream it up, that huge presence? I was not surprised, I knew perfectly well that it was the world, the world in all its nakedness which was suddenly revealing itself, and I choked with fury at that huge absurd being. You couldn't even*

> *wonder where it came from, or how it was that a world should exist rather than nothing. It didn't make sense; the world was present everywhere, in front, behind. There had been nothing before it. Nothing. There had been no moment at which it might not have existed. Naturally there was no reason for it to exist, that flowing larva. But it was not possible for it not to exist. In order to imagine nothingness, you had to be there already, right in the world, with your eyes wide open and alive. This nothingness hadn't come before existence.*[22]

According to Sartre the revelation of the being of the world to man is not a silent feature but it creates disturbance in man. It fills man with happiness or sweet disgust. This sweet disgust is combination of joy and helplessness, it is nausea. At one stroke it makes appear to man all living and non-living and particularly man's own existence in the world.

The description of being brings, into notice two questions. The first one is that of 'Knowledge' and the second one is that of nature of 'percipi and percipere'. Metaphysics in fact presupposes a theory of knowledge, every theory of knowledge in turn presupposes metaphysics. He says that, this means among other things that idealism intent on reducing being to the knowledge which we have of it, ought first to give some kind guarantee for the being of knowledge. If one begins, on the other hand, by taking the knowledge as a given, without being concerned to establish a basis for its being, and if one then affirms that ésse est percipi, the totality 'perceived-perception' lacks the support of a solid being and so falls away in nothingness.

Thus, the being of knowledge cannot be measured by knowledge, it not subject to percipi. Therefore foundation of being for the percipere and the percipi cannot itself be subject to the percipi; it must be transphenomenal. We can always agree that the percipi refers to a being not subject to the laws of appearance, but we still maintain that this transphenomenal being is the being of the subject.

Thus percipi refers to percipiens, the known to knowledge, and knowledge to the being who knows; that is knowledge refer to consciousness. This can be compared to the Noema-Noesis relation of Husserl. In This way Sartre abandons the primacy of knowledge and explains that consciousness is the knowing being in his capacity as being known.

The Consciousness

The man is consciousness but the first description goes about him in terms of consciousness as it is the base of life in a man. This life does not mean the biological but the whole life circumstances which make him a man and not just living organism. Consciousness as the basic and inner structure of man has been explained by Sartre as pre-reflective cogito and as the being of the percipere. The explanation of consciousness is linked to reflection, Cartesian cogito, percipere of Berkley and intentional consciousness of Husserl, in one or the other way. But one thing is clear in the Sartre theory of consciousness that, it is not subject to the laws of appearance, as the other domain of being is dependent on phenomenon. Consciousness makes itself appear through nausea, boredom etc., as being explained before but it itself is just a being to be intuitioned.

In his description of knowledge, Sartre explained that, the law of being in the knowing subject is to-be-conscious. This consciousness is not a mode of particular knowledge which may be called an inner meaning or self-knowledge but it is the dimension of transphenomenal being in the subject.

> *Consciousness is the knowing being in his capacity as being and not as being known. This means that we must abandon the primacy of knowledge if we wish to establish that knowledge. Of course consciousness can know and know itself. But it is itself something other than knowledge turned back upon itself.*[23]

Sartre accepts the theory of Husserl that consciousness intends or directs toward the objects. But he rejects that part of theory where Husserl says that, "All consciousness, is consciousness of something." Husserl meant by this that there is no consciousness which is not positing of a transcendent object means there is no self-conciousness or in other words the consciousness has no 'content' in itself. Sartre says that to equal the consciousness to things is to deny the cogito because It should be the first principle of philosophy to expel things from the consciousness and to establish consciousness' true connection with the world. According to Sartre consciousness as well as objects of the world such as stones, trees, buildings etc. are real existent things. So Sartre does not supports the view of Husserl that noema is unreal.

Sartre says that not all consciousness is knowledge, but all knowing consciousness mean knowledge of its object only and it is necessary at the same time that it be consciousness of itself as being that knowledge.

> *The mode of existence of consciousness is to be conscious of itself. And consciousness is consciousness of itself in so far as it is consciousness of a transcendent object. All is therefore clear and lucid in consciousness. The object with its characteristics opacity is in front of consciousness, but consciousness purely and simply consciousness of being consciousness of that object. This is the law of its existence.*[24]

We come into contact with consciousness as a basic existence which makes man a man, and not an object in the world. It is consciousness which makes knowledge possible which is knowledge of me and of the world. Now the question is what is nature of this consciousness? The Ontological structure of this consciousness can be drawn from various instances taken from the life of a man. Sartre explains that a man is separated by remaining world by a not, i.e. I am not this table, the other person is not me etc. In other words, what appears to him is that the world is separate from him. Sartre says that these negations serve as a tool to reach to myself. Being a man, in the depth of my being I know myself. It is not that I know myself from the outer world but this consciousness is my subjective state. This is consciousness of consciousness, an immediate, relation of the self to itself.

I am the knower and the remaining world is the known. But this subject-object relation has been a problem in philosophy, so Sartre explains that in order to avoid the infinite regress of introducing third term between the Knower-known, we have the ontological and epistemological necessity of introducing a law of this dyed and this is self-consciousness.

> *Consciousness of self is not dual. If we wish to avoid an infinite regress, there must be an immediate, non-cognitive relation of the self to itself.*[25]

To be conscious is to be conscious of something. Consciousness refers to and separates itself from something not itself. And to be conscious of something is to be aware of being conscious of something. But this secondary awareness is implicit in the primary consciousness of something. Sartre now explains consciousness as transcending consciousness:

> *Consciousness is a being such that in its being is in question in so far as this being implies a being other than itself.*[26]

He distinguishes types of consciousness according to psychic objects also such as pain consciousness, shame consciousness etc. but two basic distinctions are made importantly as such:

1. Unreflective consciousness, also called non-thetic consciousness or non-positional self-consciousness. This is the pre-reflective cogito. Here there is no knowledge but an implicit consciousness of being, consciousness of an object.
2. Reflective consciousness [also called thetic consciousness or positional self-consciousness]. In the sense that it transcends itself in order to reach an object.

> *Furthermore the reflecting consciousness posits the consciousness reflected-on, as its object. In the act of reflecting I pass judgment on the consciousness reflected on; I am ashamed of it, I am proud of it, I will it, I deny it etc. The immediate consciousness which I have of perceiving does not permit me either to judge or to will or to be ashamed. It does not know my perception, does not posit it; all that there is of intention I my actual consciousness is directed toward the outside, toward the world. In turn, this spontaneous consciousness of my perception is constitutive of my perceptive consciousness. In other words, every positional consciousness of an object is at the same time a non-positional consciousness of itself. Proof of this is that children who are capable of making an addition spontaneously cannot explain subsequently how they set about it.*[27]

Reflection has no primacy over the consciousness reflected on. It is not reflection which reveals the consciousness reflected on to itself but it is non-reflective consciousness which renders the reflection possible.

Sartre does not agree with Cartesian cogito which says, 'cogito ergo sum'; because Sartre puts pre-reflective cogito prior to Cartesian cogito and explains that pre-reflective cogito is the condition for Cartesian cogito. First of all, every person has consciousness of existing. This first consciousness is not positional. At one stroke it determines itself as consciousness of perception and perception both. This first self-consciousness is called non-positional consciousness of self. This self-consciousness can be considered as a mode of existence which is possible for a consciousness of something. An intention, a pleasure, a grief can exist only as an immediate self-consciousness.

Consciousness is not possible before Being, but since consciousness' being is the source and conditions of all possibility, its existence implies its essence. In his Transcendence of the Ego, Sartre describes relation of the Ego to the consciousness. He says that 'a pure consciousness' is an absolute because it is consciousness of itself. It remains a 'phenomenon' in the very special sense which explains that 'to be' and 'to appear' are one.

Thus the cogito which is performed by consciousness is oriented towards a consciousness, by a consciousness and which takes consciousness as an object. The certitude of cogito is absolute, for there is an indissoluble unity of the reflecting consciousness and the consciousness reflected upon, to the extent that the reflecting consciousness could not exist without the reflected consciousness. Sartre explains it through an example:

> *Every unreflected consciousness, being non-positional consciousness, of itself, leaves behind a non-positional memory which one can consult.*

> *For example, I was absorbed in reading a moment ago. I am now trying to recall the circumstances of my reading, my attitude, the lines that I was reading, what I am going to revive are not only those external details but also a certain density [epaisseur] of unreflected consciousness, since the objects revived could only have been perceived by this consciousness and remain relative to it. This consciousness must not be posited as an object of my reflection. I must instead direct my attention to the objects I am reviving but without losing sight of the unreflected consciousness. I must conspire with it and draw out an inventory of its content in a non-positional fashion. The outcome of this experiment is obvious: so long as I was reading, there was consciousness of the book, of the hero of the novel, but I did not inhabit this consciousness. It was only consciousness of the object and non-positional consciousness of itself. There was no I in the unreflected consciousness. When I run after a streetcar, when I look at the time, when I am absorbed in looking at a portrait, no I is present. There is consciousness of the streetcar, having to be caught and non-positional consciousness of that consciousness. On these occasions I am immersed in the world of objects. They constitute the unity of my consciousness they present themselves with values, with qualities that attract or repel, but I have disappeared, I am nothing. There is no place for me at this level of consciousness. This is not accidental; it is not due to a temporary lapse of attention, but to the structure of consciousness itself.*[28]

According to Sartre a kind of power struggle goes on between the spontaneous consciousness and the Ego. On the one hand it seems that the essential role of the Ego is to mask from consciousness its very spontaneity. On the other hand it seems that as if consciousness constituted the Ego as a false representation of itself, as if consciousness hypnotized itself with this ego it has constituted. Ego helps to make the distinction between possible and the real, between appearance and being, between the willed and the undergone. But it can happen that consciousness produces itself on the pure reflective level. Ego is there but consciousness escapes the ego on all sides, dominating and maintaining the ego by continuous creation. On this level no distinction between possible and real exists as appearance is the absolute.

Sartre says that there are no longer any barriers, nothing to conceal consciousness from itself. Then consciousness recognizes what could be called the fatality of its spontaneity, and is suddenly anguished. It is this anguish, absolute and without remedy, this fear of itself, which seems constitutive of pure consciousness. It is an anguish which is imposed upon us and which we cannot avoid. It is at one and the same time a pure event of transcendent origin and an ever possible accident of our daily life. Sartre thinks that it is consciousness which serves as a link between me and the remaining world.

> *The world has not created me, me has not created the world. They are two objects for the absolute, impersonal consciousness, and it is by this consciousness that they are linked together. This absolute consciousness, when it is purified of the I, no longer has anything of a subject. It is no longer a collection of representations. It is quite simply a primary condition and absolute source of existence. And the relation of interdependence established by this absolute consciousness between the me and the world is sufficient for the me to draw the whole content from the world.*[29]

Having defined the structures of consciousness and it nature, Sartre explains its origin in ontological sense. He says that, the man is a fact, contingent and superfluous existence thus his consciousness is also an existence. Being an ontologist, Sartre does not indulge into cause and effect of consciousness but explains that it is unwise to explain it like this. Consciousness is a 'plenum of existence', and this determination of itself by itself is an essential characteristics. That is, existence which perpetuates itself without having the force either to produce itself or to preserve itself. No knowledge can explain it why and how, as consciousness is before knowledge and Knowledge is based on it. If no prior cause can be explained, then is it possible to explain that, whether consciousness is borne from nothingness or not? Relation of consciousness and nothingness is explained by Sartre like this:

> *The existence of consciousness comes from consciousness itself. By that we need not understand that consciousness 'derives from nothingness'. There cannot be nothingness of consciousness, before consciousness. 'Before' consciousness one can conceive only of a plenum of being of which no element can refer to an absent consciousness If there is to be nothingness of consciousness there must be a consciousness which has been and which is no more and a witnessing consciousness which poses the nothingness of the first consciousness for a synthesis of recognition. Consciousness is prior to nothingness and is derived from being.*[30]

Sartre concludes about consciousness saying that ontological structure of consciousness has shown that consciousness has the structure of pre-reflective-Cogito while knowledge is based on reflection so it abandons the primacy of knowledge.

Thus Sartre discovered the being of the knower and called it absolute. The absolute here is not the result of a logical construction on the ground of knowledge but the subject of the most concrete of experiences. And it is not at all relative to this experience because it is this experience. Likewise it is a non-substantial absolute.

> *Consciousness has nothing substantial, it is pure 'appearance' in the sense that it exists only to the degree to which it appears. But it is precisely because consciousness is pure appearance because it is total emptiness (since the entire world is outside it) – it is because of this identity of appearance and existence within it that it can be considered as the absolute.*[31]

In the Nausea, Sartre explains consciousness of existence in a soliloquy:

> *I exist, it's I. The body lives all by itself, once it has started but when it comes to thought, it is I' who continue it, I who unwind it. I exist, I think, I exist. Oh how long and serpentine this feeling of existence is and I unwind it, slowly – If only I could prevent myself from thinking: I try, I succeed. My thought is me that's why I can't stop. I exist by what I think and I can't prevent myself from thinking. I exist, it's because I hate existing. It's I who pull myself from the nothingness to which I aspire: hatred and disgust for existence are just so many ways of making me exist, of thrusting me into existence. Thoughts grow and grow and here it is, huge, filling me completely and renewing my existence.*[32]

The Ontological Proof of Being

The consciousness is the ontological foundation of knowledge, the first being to whom all other appearances appear, the absolute in relation to which every phenomenon is relative. It is subjectivity itself, the immanence of self in itself. This subjective consciousness is related to the the ontological proofs to prove the Being. According to Sartre the transphenomenal being of consciousness cannot provide a basis for the transphenomenal being of the phenomenon, as he says that:

> *We have discovered transphenomenality of the being of consciousness, this very transphenomenality requires that of the being of the phenomenon. There is an ontological proof to be derived not from the reflective cogito but from the pre-reflective being of the perciepiens.*[33]

Consciousness is consciousness of something, means that transcendence is the constitutive structure of consciousness and this consciousness is supported by a being which is not itself. This is what we call ontological proof. What can properly be called subjectivity is consciousness of consciousness. But this subjectivity must be qualified in some way, and it can be qualified only as revealing intuition otherwise it is nothing. Now this revealing intuition implies something revealed. Absolute subjectivity can be established only in the face of something revealed; immanence can be defined only within the apprehension of a transcendent.

> *To say that consciousness is consciousness of something is to say that it must produce itself as a revealed-revelation of a being which is not itself and which gives itself as already existing when consciousness reveals it.*[34]

Thus the ontological proof explains that, consciousness is a being, whose existence posits its essence, and inversely it is consciousness of a being, whose essence implies its existence; that is, in which appearance lays claim to being. This Being is everywhere. Sartre owes to

Heidegger for the definition of consciousness saying that "it is a being such that in its being, its being is in question". But Sartre completes the definition and formulates as follows:

> *Consciousness is a being such that in its being, its being is in question in so far as this being implies a being other than itself.*[35]

This being is other than the transphenomenal being of phenomena and not a noumenal being which is hidden behind them. It is the being of this table, of this package of tobacco, of this lamp, more generally the being of the world, which is implied by consciousness.

> *The transphenomenal being of what exists for consciousness is itself in-itself. (lui -Meme en soi)*[36]

We can always agree that the percipi refers to a being not subject to the laws of appearance, but we still maintain that this transphenomenal being is the being of the subject. In the Nausea it is like this:

> *I am in the midst of things, which cannot be given names. Alone, wordless, defenseless, they surround me, under me, behind me, above me. They demand nothing, they don't impose themselves, they are there. Under the cushion of the seat, next to the wood, there is a thin line of shadow, a thin black line which runs along the seat with a mysterious, mischievous air, almost a smile and yet its existence is penetrating me all over, through the eyes, through the nose, through the month.*[37]
> *Everything was full, everything was active, there was no unaccented beat, everything, even the most imperceptible movement, was made of existence. Existence everywhere, to infinity, superfluous, always and everywhere; existence – which is never*

> *limited by anything but existence I slumped on the bench, dazed, stunned by that profusion of beings without origin blooming, blossoming everywhere, my ears were buzzing with existence, my very flesh was throbbing and opening, abandoning itself to the universal burgeoning, it was repulsive.*[38]

Classification of Being

Basic, ontological enquiry into the being has led to shape up the theory of being. Sartre having done away with the duality of reality and appearance established his own theory of knowledge which is dependent on consciousness, the knowing being. This consciousness served as a clue to the phenomenal world. Ontological proof explained by Sartre is the only proof which he used to describe the whole domain of being. Sartre explains that we have at each instant what Heidegger calls a pre-ontological comprehension of it. In the Nausea Sartre explains the being like this:

> *Existence is not something which allows itself to be thought of from a distance. It has to invade you suddenly, bounce upon you, weigh heavily on your heart like a huge motionless animal or else there is nothing left at all.*[39]

Sartre distinguishes two absolutely separated regions of Being as follows:

1. *The being of the pre-reflective Cogito – Being-for-itself.*
2. *The being of the phenomenon – Being-in-itself.*

Before the explanation of the for-itself, it is necessary to understand few concepts in Sarte's philosophy because the for-itself being the man is the most important part of Being and all remaining concepts find justification in the life of man. So first of all we will go through the in-itself. The for-itself will be explained in the next chapter named, 'The Human Reality'.

Being-In-Itself

This Being-in-itself is called by Sartre simply Being. Sartre's argument for its creation is against theistic creation that is creation by God. According to Sartre subject cannot get out its subjectivity to act upon transcendent being, nor without contradiction admits of the passive elements necessary in order to constitute a transcendent being arising from them. On the other hand being of phenomenon cannot act upon consciousness. Sartre takes help of the subjective structure of conciousness to explain why God as a subject cannot create the being.

> *A clear view of phenomenon of being has often been obscured by the very common prejudice which we shall call "creationism'. Since people supposed that God had given being to the world, being always appeared tainted with a certain passivity. But a creation ex-nihilo cannot explain the coming to pass of being: for if being is conceived in subjectivity, even in divine subjectivity, it remains a mode of intra-subjective being. Such subjectivity cannot have even the representation of objectivity, and consequently it cannot even be affected with the will to create the objective. Furthermore being if it is suddenly placed outside the subjective by the fulguration of which Leibniz speaks; can only affirm itself as distinct from and opposed to its creator; otherwise it dissolve in him. The theory of perpetual creation, by removing from being what the German call Selbstandigkeit, makes it disappear*

> *in the divine subjectivity. If being exists as over against God, it is its own support; it does not preserve the least trace of divine creation. In a word, even if it had been created, being-in-itself would be inexplicable in terms of creation; for it assumes its being beyond the creation.*[40]

No argument supports origin of Being-in-itself. It cannot be called causa sui in the manner of consciousness. Being is itself. It is an immanence which cannot realize itself, an affirmation which cannot affirm itself, an activity which cannot act, because it is glued to itself. Being is in-itself.

> *Being is 'in-itself', means that it does not refer to itself as self-consciousness does. It is this self. It is itself so completely that the perpetual reflection which constitutes the self is dissolved in an identity.*[41]

Being is opaque to itself because it is filled with itself. We can say that being is what it is. The special meaning which must be given to the 'is' in the phrase, being is 'what it is', is as follows; from the moment that beings exist who have to be what they are, the fact of being what they are is no longer a purely axiomatic characteristics, it is a contingent principle of being in-itself. This 'is' designates the opacity of being-in-itself. This opacity has nothing to do when related to the position of consciousness to the in-itself, it is not a kind of apprehension of it and observation of it because consciousness is without.

> *Being-in-itself has no within which is opposed to without and which is analogous to a judgment, a law, a consciousness of itself. The in-itself has nothing secret, it is solid (massif). In a sense we can designate it as a synthesis. But it is the most indissoluble of all the synthesis of itself with itself.*[42]

As being-in-itself does not enter into any connection other than itself we cannot say that being is not yet what it will be and that it is already what it is not yet. It is beyond becoming. It encompasses no negation as it is full positivity. It knows no otherness. It is itself indefinitely, exhausted in being, thus we say it is not subject to temporality.

The third characteristics of being-in-itself is that being-in-itself, 'is'. It means it can neither be derived from the possible, nor reduced to the necessary. Necessity is a relation between ideal propositions, it is not between existents. An existing phenomenon cannot be derived from another existent qua existent. Thus being-in-itself is called contingent. Possibility belongs to the for-itself, it has nothing to do with in-itself. So Sartre claims that:

> *Being-in-itself is never either possible or impossible. It is. This is what consciousness expresses in anthropomorphic terms by saying that being is superfluous (de trop). Uncreated, without reason for being, without any connection with another being, being-in-itself is de-trop for eternity.*[43]

Thus Sartre explains three characteristics of the being-in-itself.

> *1. Being is. 2. Being is in-itself. 3. Being is what it is.*[44]

It is ontological study of the objects. But in the Nausea Sartre describes it with an eye of the common man, who is trying to get into meaning of the in-itself, meaning of existence on the whole and inter-relationships of the whole world. He is unable to understand the reasons behind existents, reasons behind their abundance. Everything looks superfluous, yet things exist in their own right. It is consciousness which is thinking about them and bringing it into the world of meanings.

Trees, midnight-blue pillars, the happy bubbling of a fountain, living smells, wisps of heat haze floating in the cold air, a red haired main digesting on a bench: all these somnolences, all these digestions taken together had a vaguely comic side. Comic.... No it didn't go as far as that, nothing that exists can be comic, it was like a vague, almost imperceptible analogy with certain vaudeville situations. We were a heap of existents inconvenienced, embarrassed by ourselves, we hadn't the slightest reason for being there, any of us, each existent, embarrassed, vaguely ill at ease, felt superfluous in relation to others. Superfluous: that was the only connection I could establish between those trees, those gates, those pebbles... Each of them escaped from the relationship in which I tried to enclose it, isolated itself, overflowed. I was aware of the arbitrary nature of these relationships, which I insisted on maintaining in order to delay the collapse of the human world of measures, of quantities, of bearings; they no longer had any grip on things. Superfluous the chestnut tree, over there, opposite me, a little to the left. Superfluous, the Velleda. And I weak, languid, obscene, digesting, tossing about dismal thought – I too was superfluous. Fortunately I didn't feel this, above all I didn't understand it, but I was uneasy because I was afraid of feeling it. I dreamed vaguely of killing myself, to destroy at least one of these superfluous existences. But my death itself would have been superfluous. Superfluous my corpse, my blood on these pebbles, between these plants, in the depth of this charming park. And the decomposed flesh would have been superfluous in the earth which would have been superfluous in the earth which would have received it, and my bones, finally,

> *cleaned, stripped, neat and clean as teeth, would also have been superfluous; I was superfluous for all the times.*[45]

We can say that the description of the in-itself is neither ontologically nor phenomenologicaly possible because the in-itself is complete existence, and is called superfluous as it cannot be penetrated. Its essence implies its exixtence.

Nothingness

Sartre's concept of nothingness is interwoven with the concept of Being. The Being has been classified into two categories; the consciousness that is the man or the for-itself and the in-itself which means objects which are complete, positive and glued to itself. After defining the two regions of being Sartre goes on explaining the connection between them. He takes support from Descartes theory in this matter. Descartes tried to solve the problem of relation between the conscious and the unconscious, the soul and the body and finally found the solution in imagination, where the union of thinking substance and extended substance was effected. What Sartre adopts from Descartes is that, this relation is a synthesis. This relation, the totality which is called 'man-in-the-world' is an original emergence and it is part of the very structures of beings.

Sartre puts forward following questions to solve the trouble. He asks:

1. *What is the synthetic relation which we call being-in-the-world?*
2. *What must man and the world be in order for a relation between them to be possible?*

He says that each type of conduct, being the conduct of man in the world, can release for us simultaneously man, the world, and the relation which unites them, only on the condition that we envisage these forms of conduct as realities, objectively apprehensible and not as subjective affects, which disclose themselves only in the face of reflection. To understand the nothingness Sartre starts up his enquiry from the judgment of negation.

Origin of Negation

He sets up to the inquiry by asking a question, "Is there any conduct which can reveal the relation of man with the world"? It is obvious that every question presupposes two beings – one who questions and the one who is questioned. The question is an expectation, expecting a reply from the being. Obviously the reply will be a 'yes' or 'no'. It is the existence of these two equally objective and contradictory possibilities which on principle distinguishes the question, from affirmation or negation. It is always possible with question of this type of reply, 'Nothing' or 'Nobody' or 'Never'. So Sartre says that the possibility of a negative reply explains the transcendent fact of the non-existence of such conduct or behavior. In this way we find that a question is a bridge set-up between two non-beings. The whole process of question-answer reveals three kinds of non-beings:

1. The non-being of knowing in man.
2. The possibilities of non-being of being in transcendent being.
3. It is thus and not otherwise. It introduces a third non-being as determining the question – the non-being of limitation.

This triple non-being questions every question and in particular the metaphysical question. Now we should find a relation between being and non-being, and relation of human non-being with transcendent being. We see that this way suddenly we are encompassed with nothingness which explains that this permanent possibility of non-being, outside us and within us, conditions being and questions about being. But it cannot happen unless we 'expect' a reply.

> *Non-being always appears within the limits of human expectation. It is because I expect to find 1500 francs that I find only 1300. It is because a physicist expect a certain verification of his hypothesis that nature can tell him no. It would be in vain to deny that negation appears on the original bases of a relation to man to the world. The world does not disclose its non-being to one who has not first posited them as possibilities.*[46]

Negation is not quality of judgment according to Sartre, but it's a prejudicative attitude as this negation (non-being) is a relation of being and the judgment is only one optional expression of it.

> *The being in question is not necessarily a thinking being. If my car breaks down, it is the carburettor, the spark plugs etc., that I question. If my watch stops, I can question the watchmaker about the cause of the stopping but it is the various mechanisms of the watch that the watchmaker will in turn question. What I expect from the carburettor, what the watchmaker expects from the works of the watch, is not a judgment. It is a disclosure of being on the basis of which we can make a judgment. And if I expect a disclosure of being, I am prepared at the same time for the eventuality of a disclosure of a non-being.*[47]

Thus my question by its nature envelops a certain pre-judicative comprehension of non-being; it is in itself a relation of being with non-being, on the basis of the original transcendence; that is, in a relation of being with being. Non-being appears at the heart of being. For example, when I am supposed to meet Pierre at a café, I reach a little bit late and I don't find him. Before I say he is not here, I try to find him on the ground of nihilation of the café. It is Pierre raising himself as nothingness on the ground of the nihilation of the café. This intuitive apprehension of nothingness serves as foundation for the judgment, "Pierre is not here."

> *I myself expected to see Pierre and my expectation has caused the absence of Pierre to happen as a real event concerning this café. This example is sufficient to show that non-being does not come to things by a negative judgment; it is the negative judgment, on the contrary which is conditioned and supported by non-being.*[48]

A lot of people, who are not related to this café, cannot be told to be absent as they were not expected as being present. Their not being here just means a negation, a thought. According to Sartre negation carries no negativity in itself, category of 'not' is a positive and concrete process to brace and systematize our knowledge.

> *Negation is an abrupt break in continuity which cannot in any case result from prior affirmation. It is an original and irreducible event. Here we are in the realm of consciousness. Consciousness moreover cannot produce a negation except in the form of consciousness of negation.*[49]

Dialectical Concept of Being and Nothingness

Being and Nothingness are two complementary components of the real, which are united somehow in the production of existents, so they cannot be dealt with in isolation. Here dialectical means taking both things together or all the things in consideration, that is positive and negative for a progressive resolution into a complete theory. Sartre first of all considers the view of Hegel about 'being and nothingness'. Hegel's point of view is that:

> *Being and Nothingness constitutes two opposites, the difference between which on the level of abstraction under consideration is only a simple opinion.*[50]

Sartre denies it saying that two opposites arise as the two limiting terms of a series. They enjoy simultaneity as they are equally positive (or equally negative). But non-being is not the opposite of being, it is its contradiction. Nothingness is subsequent to being as it is being which is first posited then denied. So Being and Non-being are not concepts with the same content, as non-being is an irreducible mental act.

This point can be understood with the point that one may not affirm the being with any determination and can deny it but nobody can cause being 'not to be'. Negation cannot touch the nucleus of being of Being, as Being is absolute plenitude and entire positivity. But non-being is a negation which aims at nucleus of absolute density. Non-being is denied at the heart of Being.

Why nothingness is put subsequent to Being, Sartre answers it on the bases of use of common language. Language furnishes us with a nothingness of things and nothingness of human beings. For example we say pointing to a particular collection of objects,

> *'Touch Nothing', which means, very precisely, nothing of that collection. Similarly, if we question someone on well-determined events in his private or public life, he may reply, 'I know nothing'. And this nothing includes the totality of the facts. Even Socrates with his famous statement, "I know that I know nothing" designates by this nothing the totality of being considered as truth.*[51]

We can say that being not only has logical precedence over nothingness but also that it is from being that nothingness derives concretely its efficacy. Nothingness of being is only within the limits of being and the total disappearance of being would be disappearance of nothingness.

Phenomenological concept of Being and Nothingness

Sartre explains one more way of understanding being and nothingness; as complements. This is phenomenological concept of nothingness which is based on the concreteness of the world. Heidegger was the one to describe nothingness in relation to the concrete world. According to Heidegger, man is always separated from what he is by all the breadth of the being which he is not. He makes himself known to himself from the other side of the world and he looks from the horizon towards himself to recover his inner being. Man is 'a being of distances.' This appearance of the self beyond the world that is beyond the totality of the real is an emergence of 'human reality' in nothingness. It is in nothingness alone that being can be surpassed. At the same time, it is from the point of view of beyond the world that being is organized into the world. Thus the contingency of the world appears to human reality in so far as human reality has established itself in nothingness in order to apprehend the contingency.

Sartre's view is different from that of Heidegger's. Heidegger is wrong in assuming that it is undifferentiated emptiness or disguised otherness, that nothingness provides the ground for negation. Sartre says that in fact nothingness stands at the origin of the negative judgment because it is itself negation. Nothingness can be nothingness only by nihilating itself expressly as nothingness of the world; that is, in its nihilation it must direct itself expressly toward the world in order to constitute itself as refusal of the world. Transcendence which is 'the project of the self beyond', is far from being able to establish nothingness: on the contrary, it is nothingness which is at the very heart of transcendence and which conditions it.

Heidegger's theory of nothingness does not describe all concrete negations. Sartre's example of distance is helpful to understand his phenomenological concept of nothingness. We take two points in the space and distance between them seems as emptiness, the negativity, which separates them. Sartre states that we can use this example to describe Heidegger's point that, 'human reality' is 'remote-from-itself'; that is, that it rise in the world as that which create distances and at the same time causes them to be removed (ent-ferned). But this remoteness from self, even if it is necessary condition, in order that there may be remoteness in general, envelops remoteness in itself as the negative structure which must be surmounted.

Negation is the cement which realizes this unity. It defines precisely the immediate relation which connects these two points and which presents them to intuition as indissoluble unity of the distance. Negation is covered by measurement of the length, so negation is the raison de' etre of that measurement.

To compare distance between A and B, to that of Heidegger's distance is meant by Sartre that negations arise from concrete facts and its not that intuitive nothingness prior to concreteness. Sartre puts forward a lot of examples of the world which explain negatites and positivity within them. Absence, change, otherness, repulsion, regret, distraction etc., there is an infinite number of realities which are not only objects of judgment, but which are experienced, opposed, feared, etc., by the human being and which in their inner structure are inhabited by negation, as by a necessary condition of their existence. We shall call them negatites.

These are parts of being, dispersed in being and are not part of nothingness.He concludes by saying that nothingness can be nihilated on the foundation of being. It is neither after, nor before being, nor in a general way outside of being. Sartre says that nothingness lies coiled in the heart of being, like a worm.

Origin of Nothingness

To reach to the origin of nothingness, ontological structure of the being is required. As Sartre says that nothingness is coiled in the heart of Being like a worm, and in-itself being full positivity cannot be its origin, so the reason is to be looked for in an active being, that is the for-itself, a human-being. Structure of the nothingness itself shows that it does not nihilate itself but it is nihilated and only an active Being can nihilate itself.

> *Nothingness is not, nothingness 'is made-to-be'. Nothingness does not nihilate itself; nothingness 'is nihilated'. It follows therefore that these must exist a being (this can not be the In-itself) of which the property is to nihilate nothingness, to support it in its being, to sustain it perpetually in its very existence, a being by which nothingness comes to things. But how can this being be related to nothingness so that through it nothingness comes to things.*[52]

The being which is full positively cannot create outside itself a nothingness or transcendent being. For there should be something, by which it would surpass itself towards non-being. So it is obvious that the Being who nihilates nothingness in its being should be its own nothingness, connected with its own being:

> *The Being by which Nothingness arrives in the world is a being such that in its being, the*

nothingness of its being is in question. The being by which nothingness comes to the world must be its own nothingness.[53]

Ontological structure of the being is required to understand the origin of nihilation. Every question in essence posits the possibility of a negative reply. Every question supposes a nihilating withdrawl in relation to the given, which becomes a simple presentation, fluctuating between being and nothingness.

If the question is determined in universal determinism, it would become unintelligible and inconceivable. Determinism is based on cause effect theory. The caused being is wholly engaged by the cause in positivity, to the extent that its being depend on cause, it cannot have within itself the tiniest germ of nothingness. It is a clue to Sartre's atheism. He gives the questioner a kind of liberty to withdraw from a closed being towards nothingness. It means that, this nothingness is going to serve a crucial part in the life of a man. The question brings out the possibility of non-being from the being of questioner. This way a negative element is introduced into the world. The questioner in order to motivate himself in his being disengages himself from being. This disengagement is a human process. Thus man is the being who causes nothingness to arise in the world.

Sartre's main inquiry going along with nothingness is 'the relation of human reality to the world. When this is again questioned to this point, he relates it to the negatites which has been disclosed earlier. These negatites derive their origin from enact, expectation or a project of human being.

It is necessary that negation rises up not as a thing among other things but as the rubric of a category which presides over the arrangement and the redistribution of great masses of being in

> *things. Thus the rise of man in the midst of the being which invests him causes a world to be discovered. But the essential and primordial moment of this rise is the negation. So man is the being through whom nothingness comes to the world.*[54]

For Man, to put the whole structure of being under question and out of cause-effect series, he should view it as a totality and he must be able to put himself out of this totality. It's not annihilating the structure through human reality but the thing is that he is able to modify it from outside. This possibility of modification is freedom of man. The being of man in so far as he conditions the appearance of nothingness and this being has appeared to us as freedom. Sartre describes freedom like this:

> *Freedom as the requisite condition for the nihilation of nothingness is not a property which belongs to among others to the essence of human being. We have already noticed furthermore that with man the relation of existence to essence is not comparable to what it is for the things of the world. Human freedom precedes essence in man and makes it possible the essence of the human being is suspended in his freedom. What we call freedom is impossible to distinguish from the being of 'human reality'. Man does not exist first in order to be free subsequently. There is no difference between the being of man and his being-free.*[55]

The whole process of nihilation is a temporal process. In it against causal order consciousness engages itself in separate series. Consciousness's withdrawal is in relation to the image apprehended as subjective phenomenon. This image is to be posited as a being only as a subjective phenomenon. Sartre explains that the image must enclose in its very structure a nihilating thesis. It constitutes itself qua image while posting its object as existing elsewhere or not existing. It carries within it a double negation; First it is nihilation of the world (since the world is not offering the imagined object as an actual object of perception), secondly the nihilation of the object of the image (it is posited as not actual) and finally by the same stroke it is the nihilation of the itself (since it is not a concrete, full psychic process). Every psychic process of nihilation implies then a cleavage between the immediate psychic past and the present and this cleavage is nothingness.

A being can nihilate itself perpetually, but to the extent that it nihilate itself, it foregoes being the origin of another phenomenon, even of a second nihilation. There has been no break in continuity within the flux of the temporal development. What separates prior from the subsequent is nothing. For in every obstacle to be cleared, there is something positive which gives itself as about to be cleared.

It is necessary that conscious being constitute itself in relation to its past as separated from this past by a nothingness. It must necessarily be conscious of this cleavage in being, not as a phenomenon which it experiences, rather as a structure of consciousness. Consciousness continually experiences itself as the nihilation of its past being. Thus freedom is the human being putting his past out of play by secreting his own nothingness. It is implied that consciousness exists as a consciousness of freedom.

The man who is conscious of being and the temporal process. He is related to past and future, through a certain mode of standing, which at present can be explained as not being more not being yet. This standing has particular structure according to Sartre, which he describes as anguish. This anguish is related to freedom.

It is in anguish that man gets the consciousness

> *of his freedom, or if you prefer, anguish is the mode of being of freedom as consciousness of being: it is in anguish that freedom is, in its being, in question for itself.*[56]

Kierkegaard explains anguish saying that it's a lack in being which is characterized as anguish in the face of freedom. For Heidegger, it is apprehension of freedom. Sartre tells both of them are right, as these two conditions imply one-another: A man is surrounded by situations and these situations can affect his life. Now the anguish arises in his being to the extent that how he would be able to cope up with all the situations. So his own freedom to choose action is the heaviness on his being which is called anguish.

Every situation allows some conduct to be adopted by man and these conducts are called possibilities. According to Sartre, man should choose the best possibility. All the other possibilities should be nihilated in favour of his choice. So it is clear that possibility cannot be imposed by external causes but it is man who chooses in the situation.

> *The possibility which I make my concrete possibility can appear as my possibility only by raising itself on the bases of the totality of the logical possibilities which the situation allows.*[57]

Choosing a certain conduct as my possibility, I am there in the future and I put in my total strength for the sake of being, which I choose to be in the future. In this way a relation between my present being and future being is established and this is nothingness which has slipped in between.

> *I am not the self which I will be or I am the self which I will be in the mode of not being it. Anguish is precisely my consciousness of being my own future, in the mode of not-being.*[58]

When I recognize my possibility as my possibility, Anguish is born as I find no excuse to escape from it. My essence which had been created by me and the future which depends on my freedom makes me believe that no one can choose for me. The future being out of my reach and being only possibility also creates anguish. The freedom and possibility of man becomes a base for values, to which we call human values. As values are behavior patterns, the man is directly related to values. Sartre says that there is ethical anguish when I consider myself in original relation to values. Value derives its being from its exigency and not its exigency .Nothing justifies me choosing this or that values, it is my unique freedom which decides this or that scale of values. So my freedom is anguished at being the foundation of values while itself without foundation.

> *I am engaged in a world of values. The anguished apprehension of values as sustained in being my freedom is a secondary and mediated phenomenon. The immediate is the world with its urgency and in this world where I engage myself; my acts cause values to spring up like partridges. My indignation has given to me the negative value 'baseness, my admiration has given the positive value 'grandeur'. Above all my obedience to a multitude of taboos, which is real, reveals these taboos to me as existing in fact. The bourgeois who call themselves 'respectable citizens' do not become respectable as the result of contemplating moral values. Rather from the moment of their arising in the world they are thrown into a pattern of behavior, the meaning of which is respectability.*[59]

Man is alone in the world and feels anguish confronting the nothingness and then being engaged in the unique and original project which constitutes his being. All the barriers are nihilated by consciousness and with his absolute freedom man himself realizes the meaning of his own world and of his essence. Man cannot run from this freedom as to live in freedom is an authentic existence of man. In this way nothingness is the most important factor in man's life to make him self-sufficient.

Conclusion

We can say that the Being is as it appears through the phenomena. All the phenomena taken together in totality mean the world. Thus the world on the whole is Being and there is no hidden reality. The man as a part of Being is consciousness and lifeless objects are called the in-itself. Nothingness arises as a result of man's relation to the world. This nothingness is the intuitive apprehension of the emptiness of future possibility, when man can create his own essence through the negation of nothingness and can make value arise in the world. Nothingness serves as a clue to the Sartre's atheism.

Chapter-2
The Human Reality

The Being-For-Itself

Sartre's explanation of Being is divided into two regions. One has been explained as being-in-itself and the second one is being-for-itself. All the concepts, such as consciousness, nothingness and being-in-itself are merged together to make the concept of being-for-itself. Man as for-itself is also called the human reality.

The For-Itself as Consciousness and Nothingness

Being-for-itself is the being of percipere or the being of consciousness. So Sartre says that our study of the for-itself should have a start from pre-reflective cogito. Cogito never gives out anything other than what we ask from it. Conditions for possibility of certain types of conduct place us in a position to question the cogito about its being.

Sartre has explained about non-thetic self-consciousness that it necessarily be what it is not and not be what it is. The being of consciousness 'is a being such that in its being, its being is in question. It means that it does not coincide with itself in a full equivalence. The dialectical instrument which would serve purpose here is being-in-itself. Simply we can say Being-for-itself is not Being-in-itself.

> *The distinguishing characteristic of consciousness is that it is decompression of being. Indeed it is impossible to define it as coincidence with itself.*

> *Of this table I can say only that it is purely and simply this table. But I cannot limit myself to saying that my belief is belief; my belief is the consciousness of belief. It is often said that the act of reflection alters the fact of consciousness on which it is directed.*[60]

Consciousness is always consciousness of something. The first condition of all reflection is pre-reflective cogito. This cogito does not posit an object and remains within consciousness. But it is nonetheless homologous with the reflective cogito since it appears as the first necessity for non-reflective consciousness to be seen by itself. Sartre quotes some examples to make the point clear. He says that belief, pleasure, joy nothing can exist before being conscious. Consciousness is the measure of their being. Consciousness of belief is belief and belief is consciousness of belief.

> *The consciousness of belief and belief are one and the same being, the characteristics of which is absolute immanence. But as soon as we wish to grasp this being, it slips between our fingers and find ourselves faced with a duality with the game of reflection. For consciousness is a reflection (reflect), but qua reflection it is exactly the one reflecting (reflechissant), and if we attempt to grasp it as reflecting, it vanishes and we full back on reflection. Structure of the consciousness is reflection-reflecting.*[61]

As pre-reflective consciousness is self-consciousness, the self defines the very being of consciousness; the for-itself. The self defines the immanence of the subject in relation to himself, a way of being his own coincidence, of escaping identity and positing it as a unity, creating unstable equilibrium between identity as absolute cohesion without a trace of diversity and unity as a synthesis of multiplicity. This is what is called presence to itself. This presence to itself is the point where nothingness steps in the structure of the for-itself.

Presence to itself is different from the principle of identity. Presence of being to itself implies a detachment on the part of being in relation to itself while principle of identity is veritable plenitude of being because there is left no place for any negativity. Presence to self, supposes that an impalpable fissure has slipped into being. If being is present to itself it means it is not wholly itself Presence supposes separation. And this separation of subject from himself is 'nothing'.

The fissure within consciousness is a nothing except for the fact that it denies and that it can have being only as we do not see it. Sartre explains that the negative which is the nothingness of being and the nihilating power both together, is nothingness. Everywhere else in one way or another we must confer on it being-in-itself as nothingness. But the nothingness which arises in the heart of consciousness is not. It is made to be. Belief for example, is not the contiguity of one being with another being; it is its own presence to itself, its own decompression of being. Otherwise the unity of the for-itself would dissolve into the duality of the two in-itself. Thus the for-itself must be its own nothingness.

> *The being of consciousness qua consciousness is to exist a distance from itself as a presence to itself, and this empty distance which being carries in its being is nothingness. Thus in order for a self to exist, it is necessary that the unity of this being include its own nothingness as the nihilation of identity. The for-itself is the being which determines itself to exist in as much as it cannot coincide with itself.*[62]

Nothingness cannot be found if there is no conducting thread in the consciousness. It means that only in non-reflective cogito nothingness is not possible; as nothingness is always an elsewhere.

It is the obligation for the for-itself never to exist except in the form of an elsewhere in relation to itself, to exist as a being which perpetually effects in itself a break in being. This break does not refer us elsewhere to another being; it is only a perpetual reference of the self to self, of the reflection to the reflecting, of the reflecting to the reflection.

Thus coming out of for-itself from the whole of being is presented by Sartre saying that nothingness is the hole in being, this fall of the in-itself towards the self, the fall by which the for-itself is constituted. But this nothingness be made-to-be if its borrowed existence is correlative with a nihilating act on the part of being. This perpetual act by which the in-itself degenerates into presence to itself we shall call an ontological act.

> *Nothingness comes to being only through a particular being which is human reality.*[63]

Human reality is the being in so far as within its being and for its being it is the unique foundation of nothingness at the heart of being. Yet we may say, even if it is a being which is not what it is and which is what it is not. It means that the nothingness which is in the heart of for-itself, causes in turn something positive, as distance causes measurements to happen. This way this nothingness is purposive. So far having explained the in-itself, nothingness and consciousness, it can be said certainly about the for-itself which is human reality that it is 'Being-for-itself (etre-pour-soi)'.

> *The nihilation of being-in-itself; conscious-ness conceived as a lack of being, a desire for being a relation to being. By bringing nothingness into the world the for-itself can standout from being and judge other beings by knowledge what it is*

> *not. Each for-itself is the nihilation of a particular being.*[64]

The For-itself and Bad Faith

To be in anguish means to be conscious of one's freedom and to be engaged alone with one's future. Thus to sustain anguish in the being is not easy and man always likes to choose easier way out. To live in anguish means to engage every moment of life in freedom and choosing in a right way. It also includes acceptance of failures, depressions with responsibility and without escape. But it is tough to go with such a heavy responsibility so man chooses escape that is called flight. There are different patterns of flight. One is starting to believe in determinism. We do not go for looking at all the possibilities but depend on the one chosen as if it has been imposed on us from without. We introduce in ourselves the possibility of in-itself. We deny to admit that we have chosen but we ourselves believe that it was the only way out chosen for us. Thus we flee from anguish by attempting to apprehend ourselves from without as an other or as a thing.

> *It is reflective conduct with respect to anguish; it asserts that there are within us antagonistic forces whose type of existence is comparable to that of things. It attempts to fill the void which encircles us, to re-establish the links between past and present, between present and future. It provides us with a nature productive of our acts, and these very acts it makes transcendent; it assigns to them a foundation in something other than themselves by endowing them with an inertia and externality eminently reassuring because they constitute a permanent game of excuses.*[65]

Anguish, flight both of them are in the some

consciousness. And it is not possible to flee from something without being aware of it before flight the for-itself is aware of anguish, the cause of flight. Sartre explains that:

> *I must of necessity perpetually carry within me what I wish to flee but also that I must aim at the object of my flight in order to flee it. This means that anguish, the intentional aim of anguish, and a flight from anguish towards reassuring myths must all be given in the unity of same consciousness. In a word, I flee in order not to know but I cannot avoid knowing that I am fleeing. And the flight from anguish is only a mode of becoming conscious of anguish. Thus anguish properly speaking can be neither hidden nor avoided.*[66]

This anguish gives way to two modes of conduct. One is freedom and the other is 'bad faith'. Relation of bad-faith to anguish is not the right course of action chosen by man, but man is found engaged in bad-faith most of the time. According to Sartre one determined and essential attitude of human reality in which consciousness instead of directing its negation outward turns it toward itself, is called bad-faith (Mauvaise-foi).

A bad faith is a lie to oneself within the unity of single consciousness. The term is used for the phenomenon wherein one denies one's total freedom and chooses to behave as an inert object. Bad faith rests on a vacillation between transcendence and facticity which refuses to recognize either one for what it really is or to recognize them. It is closely related to self-deception and Friedrich Nietzsche's concept of resentment.

The man being free is condemned to choose, he cannot escape this freedom, even in overwhelming circumstances. As man is capable of exercising his freedom in every instance of life, for this reason, man chooses in anguish. Bad-faith is not to expel this anguish but to surpass the nothingness which a man is in relation to himself. Now man is in the presence of two human ekstases: the ekstasis which throws man into being-in-itself and the ekstasis which engages man in non-being. Behavior of man in the face of being-in-itself, when questioned, it presupposes that he is not this being. Sartre starts up his enquiry from anguish like this:

> *Yet to flee anguish and to be anguish cannot be exactly the same thing. If I am anguish in order to flee it, that presupposes that I can decenter myself in relation to what I am, that I can be anguish in the form of "not being it that I can dispose of a nihilating power at the heart of anguish itself. This nihilating power nihilates anguish in so far as I flee it and nihilates itself in so far as I am anguish in order to flee it. This attitude is what we call Bad Faith.*[67]

As bad faith is associated with nothingness and nothingness directly engages freedom so this conduct is to be found in freedom only. We can say that In bad-faith we are anguish-in-order-to-flee-anguish within the unity of a single consciousness. If Bad-faith is to be possible, we should be able within the same consciousness to meet with the unity of being and non-being, the being-in-order-not-to-be. Sartre says that the for-itself must be capable of his own nothingness; that is, he can be at the origin of non-being in being only if his being in himself and by himself is paralyzed with nothingness. Thus the transcendences of past and future appear in the temporal being of human reality. But bad-faith is instantaneous. So consciousness must be in the instantaneity of the pre-reflective cogito if the human being is to be capable of Bad-faith.

> *The human being is not only the being by whom negatites are disclosed in the world; he is also the*

> *one who can take negative attitudes with respect to himself.*[68]

Bad faith is identified with falsehood. Bad faith is a lie to oneself, on condition that we distinguish the lie to oneself from lying in general. In general lying, negation does not bear on consciousness itself: it aims only at the transcendent. Essence of lie is that liar himself knows the truth which he is hiding from the other. So ideal description of the liar is, a cynical consciousness, affirming truth within himself, denying it in words, and denying that negation as such. The fact expressed is transcendent since it does not exist, and the original negation rests on a truth; that is on a particular type of transcendence. As for the inner negation which is related to the affirmation for myself of truth, this rests on words; that is on an event in the world.

> *The inner disposition of the liar is positive; it could be the object of an affirmative judgment. The liar intends to deceive and he does not seek to hide his intention from himself nor to disguise the translucency of consciousness; on the contrary he has recourse to it when there is a question of deciding secondary behavior. It explicitly exercises a regulatory control over all attitudes.*[69]

Thus the lie does not put into play the inner structure of present consciousness. All the negations bear an object as an aim away from consciousness. So the lie does not need an ontological foundation.

But the duality of the deceiver and the deceived does not exist in bad faith. In bad faith it is from myself that I am hiding the truth. Bad faith does not come from outside the human reality, but consciousness affects itself with bad faith.

> *There must be an original intention and project of bad-faith; this project implies a comprehension*

> *of bad-faith as such and a pre-reflective apprehension (of) consciousness as affecting itself with bad faith.*[70]

The man who is affected with bad faith must be conscious of it since the being of consciousness is consciousness of being. It appears that I must be in good-faith, at least to the extent that I am conscious of my bad-faith. But willing and cynical attempt would be failure of bad faith. Actually it constitutes itself well within the projects as its very condition. Thus bad faith vacillates between good faith and cynicism.

> *Bad-faith presents an autonomous and durable form It can even be the normal aspect of life for a great number of people. A person can live in bad-faith, which does not mean that he does not have abrupt awakenings to cynicism or to good faith, but which implies a constant and particular style of life.*[71]

People use censor of passport, customs, currency control etc. to take recourse to bad-faith. Instincts, individual drives etc. so much affect consciousness of person as being reality as the table is a table in reality and people take them as real psychic facts in way of choosing. Subject is related to the phenomena as the deceived to the behavior of the deceiver.

Thus it is in the translucency of the consciousness that everything happens and the structure of consciousness shows that it is aware of itself. Being without, objective facts and phenomena cannot affect consciousness for bad-faith, as bad faith is related to pre-reflective consciousness.

Patterns of Bad Faith:

Sartre explains two patterns of bad faith. They are as follows:

1. Transcendence-Facticity Pattern: This pattern is explained by Sartre with an example of a lady, on date with a friend. During discussions lady is well aware of the physical advances he makes but she pretends to behave as an inert object under the name of respect and dignity. She herself carries the same desire in heart but to decide freely the acts according to her desires would be humiliating so she does not apprehend the desire. He takes her hand. To consent is to engage herself and to withdraw is to break the harmony. So she postpones the moment as long as possible. She leaves her hand inert, using intellect she talks about other things and let man make advances ignoring it. Here is double attitude, divorce of the body from soul is accomplished. This woman is in bad-faith. She reduced the actions of her companion existing in the mode of the in-itself. She herself enjoys the desire in its transcendence. She makes her body a passive object to which events can happen but which can neither provoke them nor avoid them because all possibilities are outside of it.

> *It is a certain art of forming contradictory concepts which unite in themselves both an idea and the negation of that idea. The basic concept which is thus engendered utilizes the double property of the human being who is at once a facticity and a transcendence. These two aspects of human reality are and ought to be capable of a valid coordination. But bad faith does not wish either to coordinate them or to surmount them in a synthesis. Bad faith seeks to affirm their identity while preserving their differences. It must affirm facticity as being transcendence and transcendence as being facticity. In such a way that at the instant when a person apprehends the one, he can find himself abruptly with the other.*[72]

In normal life there are various instances when man is in bad-faith in the form of facticity-transcendence pattern. Love relationship is such an example when there is contact of two people in facticity while they seek unity in the transcendence. Sartre cites various examples from writing titles as; River of fire, Longing for infinite, Plato's error, Lawrence's deep cosmic intuition etc.

Here we leave facticity to find ourselves suddenly beyond the present factual condition of man, beyond the psychological, in the heart of Metaphysics. "He has become what he was" or "Eternity at last changes each man into himself" etc., these formulas have only the appearance of bad faith. Showing our transcendence changed into facticity, is the source of infinity of excuses for our failures or our weaknesses. The concept of transcendence–facticity is one of the most basic instruments of bad-faith.

2. ***Being-in-itself Pattern:*** There is one more pattern of bad-faith. Another kind of duplicity derived from human reality and that is its being-for-itself implies complementarily a being-for-others. Being-for-others means the equal dignity of being, possessed by my being-for-others and by my being-for-myself, permits a perpetually disintegrating synthesis and a perpetual game of escape from the for-itself to the for-others and from the for-others to the for-itself.

The truth of human-reality is to be a being which is what it is not and which is not what it is. So to behave as an object is not authentic human life and is a pattern of bad faith. The idea of sincerity (it's a demand and not a state), the antithesis of bad-faith, will be very instructive in the connection that these ideas of disintegration appear to consciousness and come in existence. According to Sartre what should a human be, is like this:

> *If man is what he is, bad faith is forever impossible and candor ceases to be his ideal and becomes instead his being. ... If candor or sincerity is a universal value, it is evident that the maxim "one must be what one is" does not serve solely as a regulating principle for judgments and concepts by which I express what I am. It posits not merely an ideal of knowing but an ideal of being. It proposes for us an absolute equivalence of being with itself as a prototype of being. In this sense it is necessary that we make ourselves what we are. But what are we then if we have the constant obligation to make ourselves what we are, if our mode of being is having the obligation to be what we are?*[73]

This pattern of behaving as an in-itself is explained by Sartre with an example of a waiter in a café who applies himself to chaining his movements as if they were mechanisms. There are other examples of the grocer, of the tailor, of the auctioneer, by which they endeavor to persuade their clientele that they are nothing but a grocer, an auctioneer, a tailor because a grocer who dreams is offensive to the buyer. There are indeed many precautions to imprison a man in what he is, as if we live in a condition that he might escape from it, that he might break away and suddenly elude his condition.

> *The waiter in the café cannot be immediately a café waiter in the sense that this inkwell is an inkwell, or the glass is a glass. It is by no means that he cannot form reflective judgments or concepts concerning his condition.*[74]

Sartre explains that cafe waiter is very well aware of his rights and duties as a waiter but there is no common measure between his being and Mime (waiter in question). He attempts to realize a being-in-itself of the cafe waiter. He fulfills every condition to be that but this conduct is not possible .A man cannot be in the mode of being-in-itself thus he is a waiter in the mode of being what he is not. It means that it is not in the nature of man to be in-itself.

We are dealing with more than mere social positions. Sartre says that I am never any one of my attitudes, any one of my actions. I cannot say either that I am here or that I am not here, In the sense that we say that box of matches is on the table: this would be to confuse my 'being-in-the-world' with a 'being-in-the-midst-of-the-world'. Nor that I am standing, nor that I am seated: this would be to confuse my body with the idiosyncratic totality of which it is only one of the structures. On all sides I escape being and yet I am.

Whatever is the pattern, In bad faith man not only denies the qualities which he possesses and sees himself as the being he is for example, being a coward, he not only apprehends 'not being cowardly' but also tries to constitute himself as a being which he is not. For example he apprehends himself as being courageous which he is not. Necessarily I am not courageous that's why bad faith is bad faith. If I were courageous I would be in good faith. Bad faith attempts to constitute myself as being what I am not.

> *It is particularly requisite that the very negation of being should be itself the object of a perpetual nihilation, that the very meaning of 'non-being' be perpetually in question in human reality. If I were not courageous in the way in which this inkwell is not a table; that is, If I were isolated in my cowardice, propped firmly against it, incapable of putting it in relation to its opposite, If I were not capable of determining myself as cowardly that is to deny courage to myself and thereby to escape my cowardice in the very moment that I posit it, if it were not on principle impossible for*

> *me to coincide with my not-being-courageous as well as with my being-courageous then any project of bad faith would be prohibited to me. Thus in order for bad faith to be possible, sincerity itself must be in bad-faith. The condition of the possibility for bad-faith is that human reality, in its most immediate being, in the intra-structure of the pre-reflective Cogito, must be what it is not and not be what it is.*[75]

The 'Faith' of Bad Faith

The true problem of bad faith stems evidently from the fact that bad faith is faith. It cannot be either a cynical lie or certainty, If certainty is the intuitive possession of the object. But if we take belief as meaning the adherence of being to its object when the object is not given or is given indistinctly, then bad faith is belief; and the essential problem of bad faith is a problem of belief.

If bad faith is represented as bad faith it would be cynicism; If believed as sincerity it would be good-faith, so to be in bad faith is not giving it any name. It's a kind of attitude which believes in-itself. Bad faith does not hold the norms and criteria of truth as they are accepted by the critical thought of good faith but it decides the nature of truth for itself. In Bad faith a truth appears as a certain kind of thinking, a type of being; similar to that of objects.

Ontological structure of bad faith explains that a being in bad-faith is what it is not, and not what it is. In bad faith a peculiar type of evidence appears, that is, non-persuasive evidence. Bad faith apprehends evidence but it is resigned in advance to not being fulfilled by this evidence, to not being persuaded and transformed into good faith. This original project of bad faith is a decision in bad faith on the nature of faith. There is no question of a reflective, voluntary decision, but of a spontaneous determination of our being.

Non-thetic consciousness is not to know but it is in the translucency at the origin of all knowing. At the same time the law of pre-reflective cogito implies that the being of believing ought to be consciousness of believing. The ideal of good-faith (to believe what one believes) is, like that of sincerity (to be what one is), an ideal of being-in-itself. Every belief is a being which questions its being, which can realize itself only in its destruction, which can manifest itself to itself only by denying itself. Consequently the primitive project of bad-faith is only the utilization of this self-destruction of the fact of consciousness. If every belief in good-faith is an impossible belief then there is a place for every impossible belief.

> *In willing this self-destruction of belief, from which science escapes by searching for evidence, it ruins the beliefs which are opposed to it, which reveals themselves as being only belief. Thus we can better understand the original phenomenon of bad-faith.*[76]

My inability to believe that I am courageous will not discourage me since every belief involves not quite believing. I shall define this impossible belief as my belief. So it is clear that being based on basic concept of non-thetic consciousness and on good-faith there is no cynical lie and knowing preparation for deceitful concepts. But the first act of Bad-faith is flight. To flee what it cannot flee, to flee what it is. The very project of flight reveals to bad faith an inner disintegration in the heart of being, and it is this disintegration which bad faith wishes to be.

The nature of being and its immediate relation with the in-itself, actually conditions there two immediate attitudes in the face of being which are called good-faith and bad-faith. Good-faith seeks to flee the inner disintegration of being in the direction of the in-itself which it should be and is not. Bad faith seeks to flee the in-itself by means of the inner disintegration of being. But it denies this very disintegration as it denies that it is itself bad-faith.

> *It denies itself as bad-faith and aims at the in-itself which I am not in the mode of 'not-being-what-one-is-not'. If bad-faith is possible, it is because it is an immediate, permanent threat to every project of the human being; it is because consciousness conceal in its being a permanent risk of bad-faith. The origin of this risk is the fact that the nature of consciousness simultaneously is to be what it is not and not to be what it is.*[77]

The Facticity of the For-Itself

If man is to be understood, this can be done with reference to his present conditions and surroundings. Sartre says that presence of man in the world makes him realize that he is in a situation. The for-itself is in the manner of an event, as Philip-II has been, or that my friend Pierre is or exists. These conditions are not chosen by the for-itself in which he appears by birth. Sartre calls it to be thrown into the world and abandoned in the 'situation'. For example-Pierre is a French bourgeois in 1942, Schmitt was a Berlin Worker in 1870. It is called by Sartre the facticity or contingency of the for-itself.

> *It is as pure contingency in as much as for it as for things in the world, as for this wall, this tree, this cup, the original question can be posited: Why is this being exactly such and not otherwise? It is in so far as there is in it something of which it is not the foundation its presence to the world.*[78]

Metaphysical approach to find reasons for this facticity are obvious as he says that Being apprehends itself as not being its own foundation, and this apprehension is at the basis of every cogito. He mentions about Descartes:

> *Descartes wants to profit from this revelation, he apprehends himself as an imperfect being "since he doubts", but in this imperfect being, he establishes the idea of perfection.... the being which possesses in itself the idea of perfection cannot be its own foundation, for if it were, it would have produced itself in conformance with that idea.*[79]

Descartes apply this idea of perfection to the existence of God. Sartre uses this discrepancy, which is between a perfect idea and the imperfect man, against Descartes. He explains that this apprehension of being as a lack of being is first a comprehension on the part of the cogito of its own contingency, and it is our own apprehension of ourselves as we appear to ourselves as having the character of an unjustifiable act. In the novel Nausea Sartre explains contingency, when in an effort to understand himself and the objects of world he understands what is existence and its reason.

> *The essential thing is contingency. I mean that, by definition, existence is not necessity. To exist is simply to be there; what exists appears, lets itself be encountered, but you can never deduce it. People have tried to overcome this contingency by inventing a necessary, causal being. But no necessary being can explain existence: contingency is not an illusion, an appearance which can be dissipated; it is absolute and consequently perfect gratuitousness.*[80]

Sartre compares his idea of feeling contingent to that of feeling of guilt of Heidegger. Heidegger's theory, 'from unauthentic to authentic', describes restlessness and an appeal to the conscience (*Ruf des Gewissens*), a feeling of guilt.

> *In truth Heidegger's description shows all too clearly his anxiety to establish an ontological foundation for an ethics with which he claims not to be concerned, as also to reconcile his humanism with the religious sense of the transcendent. The intuition of our contingency is not identical with a feeling of guilt. Nevertheless it is true that in our own apprehension of ourselves, we appear to ourselves as having the character of an unjustifiable fact.*[81]

When the for-itself finds himself as consciousness, he comes across nothingness, and again when he tries to discover reasons for its facticity he again comes across nothingness. According to Sartre for the for-itself to found its own being, it would have to exist at a distance from itself and that would imply a certain nihilation of being, founded as of the being which founds duality, which would be unity. So whenever we try to find foundation for this being, we would find it as 'contingent as being-in-itself' and foundation of its own 'nothingness'. When the for-itself tries to find God as causa sui, then by a nihilating act he returns to the self, like recovery of the self by the self. The original relation of necessity is a return to self, reflexivity.

> *The original necessity in turn appears on the foundation of a contingent being, precisely that being which is in order to be the cause of itself.*[82]

Leibniz says that necessary is a being whose possibility implies its existence. It implies that possibility precedes existence. Sartre explains that it is possible in thought only. Here being unrolls from possibility like a consequence from principle. But possibility is after existence. Ontological structure of the real explains possibility in a different way. As we have gone through the theory that nothingness gives way to freedom and freedom to possibility. The possibility our making ourselves the way we want to be. This is our inner possibility. As far as outer possibility is concerned, as we say "it is possible that Pierre is dead", we need a witness concerning this. Being has its possibility outside of itself in the pure regard which gauges its chances of Being.

> *Possibility appears to us as an ontological structure of the real. Then it belongs to certain beings as their possibility it is the possibility which they are, which they have to be. In this case being sustains its own possibilities in being: it is their foundation, and the necessity of being cannot then be derived from its possibility. In a word, God, if he exists, is contingent.*[83]

Sartre concludes that being of consciousness; that is, for-itself is contingent. Role of consciousness is to be found its being through the act of nihilation and not to give being to itself or to receive it from others. God's existence cannot be established either as necessary or as possible. Facticity of the for-itself, produces a desire to search for a foundation but explicative link with the real foundation cannot be established.

> *The for-itself is the in-itself losing itself as in-itself in order to find itself as consciousness. Thus consciousness holds within itself its own being-as-consciousness, and since it is its own nihilation, it can refer only to itself.*[84]

Sartre says that the In-itself cannot provide the foundation for anything. It does so by giving itself the modification of the for-itself. The whole Idea of foundation comes into the world through the for-itself. The in-itself, engulfed and nihilated in the absolute event which is the appearance of the foundation or upsurge of the for-itself, remains at the heart of the for-itself as its original contingency. He explains it through an example of thirst, when the in-itself in the form of water and glass is nihilated by the for-itself. I can ask myself, "Why am I thirsty? Why am I conscious of this glass? Of this me?" When I consider this totality as in-itself, it nihilates itself under my regard. I return to for-itself, apprehended in its suggestion of duality as the foundation of itself. Thirst is related to man but its satisfaction is like a feeling of contingency for him.

> *The for-itself is sustained by a perpetual contingency for which it assumes the responsibility and which it assimilates without ever being of the in-itself which, without ever allowing itself to be apprehended, haunts the for-itself and reattaches it to being-in-itself, this contingency is what we shall call the facticity of the for-itself. It is this facticity which permits us to say that the for-itself is, that it exists, although we can never realize the facticity, and although we always apprehend it through the for-itself.*[85]

Sartre states that man can always give meaning to the obligations which his state involves. Although the facticity is given but man is still responsible for himself. We can choose meaning of the situation but not the situation itself. This is the result of the fact that while I must play at being a café waiter in order to be one, it would be in vain for me to play at being a diplomat or sailor, for I would not be one. This fact of life is inapprehensible. So choosing the meaning of situation as foundation of one's being, causes me to apprehend myself simultaneously as totally responsible for my being.

> *It is not even strictly speaking a resistance of fact since it is only by recovering it in the substructure of the pre-reflective Cogito that I confer on it its meaning and its resistance.*

> *Facticity is only one indication which I give to myself of the being to which I must reunite myself in order to be what I am.*[86]

The for-itself looking deep into itself as the consciousness of being there will discover motivations : that is, it will be perpetually referred to itself and to its constant freedom. But facticity paralyzes these motivations. Thus Sartre says that the relation of the for-itself to facticity can be correctly termed as 'factual necessity'. The for-itself is conscious of its facticity. It has the feeling of its complete gratuity. It apprehends itself as being there for nothing as being de trop.

This contingency or facticity of the for-itself is in-itself, which he wishes to remove, to gain its own being. Here the in-itself is nihilated in the gain of the self through a reflective act because the for-itself is always aware of its unjustifiable presence in the world.

The For-itself and the Being of Value

The study of human reality must begin with the cogito. Temporality, possibilities, understanding, everything has importance with reference to cogito. Sartre explains that the for-itself which carries nihilation in its heart, cannot sustain this nihilation without determining itself a lack of being. This is not just emptiness but it carries a certain structure in itself which is of a purposive nature. This lack defines the for-itself as it gives it a value.

> *An external being has not expelled the in-itself from consciousness: rather the for-itself is perpetually determining itself not to be the in-itself. This means that it can establish itself only in terms of the in-itself and against the in-itself.*[87]

Here nihilation is the connecting bond between for-itself and in-itself. On the one hand for-itself decide not to be in-itself and nihilates it. Through the transcending act it tries to discover the total, out of reach presence of the in-itself.

> *It is precisely the nihilation which is the origin of transcendence conceived as the original bond between the for-itself and the in-itself.*[88]

Lack is the most penetrating negation of human reality. It cannot belong to the in-itself as it is all positivity. It appears in the world only with the upsurge of human reality. The being which is released to the intuition of human reality is always that to which something is lacking, i.e. existing.

> *If I say that the moon is not full and that one quarter is lacking, I base this judgment on full intuition of the crescent moon. Thus what is released to intuition is an in-itself which by itself is neither complete nor incomplete but which simply is what it is, without relation with other beings. In order for this in-itself to be grasped as the crescent moon, it is necessary that a human reality surpasses the given toward the project of the realized totality. Here the disc of the full moon.*[89]

Lacking is posited as that whose synthetic addition to the existing will reconstitute the synthetic totality of the lacked. In this lacking is of the same nature as the existing.

> *This lacking as the complement of existing is determined in its being by the synthetic totality of the lacked. Thus in the human world the incomplete being which is released to intuition as lacking is constituted in its being by the lacked – that is, by what it is not. It is the full moon which confers on the crescent moon its being as crescent; what is not determines what is.*[90]

Human reality which is a lack, can surpass being towards the lack. Existence of desire as a human fact proves that human reality is a lack. Desire resides neither in the outside world nor in the consciousness. It's a way by which consciousness relates itself to the objects of the world. For the desire to be able to be desire to itself, it must necessarily be itself transcendence; that is it must by nature be an escape from itself toward the desired object. In other words, it must be a lack.

> *Desire is a lack of being. It is haunted in its inmost being by the being of which it is desire. Thus it bears witness to the existence of lack in the being of human reality.*[91]

According to Sartre the for-itself founds itself in negation, it means that it denies a certain being or mode of being in relation to itself. What it denies is being-in-itself but as this nihilation is its own nihilation, the denial in relation to itself can be only of itself. So Sartre concludes that 'the self-as-being-in-itself' is what human reality lacks and it gives meaning to human reality.

As the for-itself is never complete, this basic structure of for-itself is like this, that it cannot find in-itself as lacking. But this failure causes the for-itself to rise from in-itself as the foundation of its own nothingness. This failure gives being to the for-itself. The for-itself is a perpetual striving toward the goal which is the missing in-itself thus Sartre says that this failure has meaning only when for-itself apprehends itself as failure in the presence of being which it has failed to be.

> *Such is the origin of transcendence. Human reality in its own surpassing (transcendence) towards what it lacks; it surpasses itself towards the particular being which it would be if it were what it.*[92]

Human reality, when it comes into existence grasps itself as a lack of being. Throughout life it works on to fill-up this lack. Here Sartre gives example of second Cartesian proof; which says that the imperfect being surpasses itself towards perfect being; the being which is foundation only of its nothingness surpasses itself toward the being which is the foundation of its being. Thus says Sartre that the being toward which human reality surpasses itself is not a transcendent God; it is at the heart of human reality; it is only human reality itself as totality and in other words the man seeks completion of its own self.

Thus human reality arises as such in the presence of its own totality or self as a lack of that totality. Sartre says that it is impossible to attain this totality, as it cannot be given by nature because it combines in itself the incompatible characteristics of the in-itself and the for-itself. But a further movement of thought establish this being and absolute absence of this totality as transcendence beyond the world resulting in the name of God.

> *The being of human reality is suffering because it rises in being as perpetually haunted by a totality which it is without being able to be it, precisely because it could not attain the in-itself without losing itself as for-itself. Human reality therefore is by nature an unhappy consciousness with no possibility of surpassing its unhappy state.* [93]

The being towards which consciousness surpasses itself is not transcendent God but the concrete one, as consciousness is concrete. The most important thing here is that the completion which a for-itself seeks is his subjective state and not an objective reality. Because this being comes into the world along with the consciousness and the for-itself and consciousness are one. This concrete consciousness arises in a situation to which this concrete consciousness, the self is present. As the lack in the for-itself itself as in-itself so the self is individual; it is the individual completion of the self which haunts the for-itself. In this way the lack explains the atheism of Sartre and establishs the for-itself in original relation to the values. So human-reality is that by which value arises in the world. Being of value is that towards which a being surpasses its being. It means that value is beyond acts, beyond being. Value haunts freedom. It means that relation of value to the for-itself is very peculiar, because in its being it makes itself be as having to be this being. The self, the for-itself and their inter-relation stand within the limits of an unconditioned freedom, in the sense that nothing makes value exist, unless it is that freedom which by the for-itself exists within the limits of concrete facticity.

Values do not appear with non-thetic self-consciousness but it is with regard to reflective act of consciousness that values are given weightage. The reflective consciousness can be called moral consciousness since it cannot arise without at the same moment disclosing values. I am free in my reflective consciousness to direct my attention on the values or neglect them.

The For-itself and the Being of Possibilities

Possibilities arise out of lack of human-reality. The original transcendent relation of the for-itself to the self perpetually outlines a project of identification of the for-itself with an absent for-itself which it is and which it lacks. This identification is related to a peculiar possibility of the for-itself because what is given as the peculiar lack of each for-itself and what is strictly defined as lacking to precisely this for-itself and no other, is the individual possibility of the for-itself.

The possible rises on the ground of the nihilation of the for-itself. It is not conceived thematically afterwards as a means of reuniting the self. Rather the upsurge of the for-itself as the nihilation of the in-itself and the decompression of being causes possibility to arise as one of the aspects of this decompression of being; that is as a way of being what one is, at a distance from the self. Thus the for-itself cannot appear without being haunted by value and projected toward its own possibilities.

The possible comes into the world through human reality. Just as there can be lack in the world only if it comes to the world through a being which in its own lack, so there can be possibility in the world only if it comes through a being which is for-itself in its own possibility. The other part of the being, the In-itself being a fullness, cannot have possibilities. In-itself is related to possibility through its relation with the for-itself. The possibility of being stopped by a fold in the cloth belongs neither to the billiard ball which rolls nor to the cloth; it can arise only in the organization into a system of the ball and the cloth by a being which has a comprehension of possibilities.

> *To comprehend possibilities qua possibility or to be its own possible is one and the same necessity for the being such that in its being, its being is in question.*[94]

The possible is an absence constitutive of consciousness is so far as consciousness itself makes itself. For example, thirst is thirst when it makes itself thirst. It is haunted by the presence of the self of thirst itself. Thirst as a concrete value is related to a lacking for-itself, which would realize it as satisfied thirst and confers on it being-in-itself. This missing for-itself is 'possible'.

Desire perpetuate itself, man clings ferociously to his desires. Wish of desire is a filled emptiness but one which shapes its repletion as a mould shapes the bronze which has been poured inside it. So the possible of the consciousness of thirst is the consciousness of drinking.

But coincidence with self is impossible. The for-itself even after realization of the possible is for-itself, with another horizon of possibilities. For-itself is separated from its presence to itself with which it lacks and which is its own possibility, In one sense separated by nothing and in another sense by a totality of the existent in the world.

The For-itself and the Circuit of Selfness

The being beyond which the for-itself projects the coincidence with itself is the world as distance of infinite being, beyond which man must be united with his possible. Sartre used here the expression circuit of selfness (circuit de ipseite):

> *We shall use the expression circuit of selfness for the relation of the for-itself with the possible which it is, and "World" for the totality of being in so far as it is traversed by the circuit of selfness.*[95]

He says that possibility is not only thematically posited but it is outlined beyond the world and gives to present perception its meaning, as this possibility is apprehended in the real world in the circuit of selfness. Sartre takes example of thirst; he says that the non-reflective consciousness of thirst is apprehended by means of the glass of water as desirable, without putting the self in the centripetal position as the end of the desire. But the possible repletion appears as a non-positional correlate of the non-thetic consciousness on the horizon of the glass-in-the-midst-of-the-world.

Circuit of selfness belongs to the relation between for-itself and the world. Sartre mentions of the ego at this point and says that ego does not belong to the domain of for-itself. Reason of the transcendence of the ego is that its 'I' is not a mode of for-itself but its unifying pole is in-itself. 'I' is always given as having been there before consciousness, to be revealed gradually.

> *The ego appears to consciousness as a transcendent in-itself, as an existent in the human world, not as of the nature of consciousness.*[96]

It is not ego which serves as a personalizing pole of impersonal consciousness but it is consciousness in its fundamental selfness which allows the appearance of the ego as the transcendent phenomenon of that selfness. What makes consciousness personal is the pure nihilating movement of reflection. Self thus cannot inhabit the consciousness. So the ego which is sign of the personality does not confer personal existence on the being but it is the fact that the being exists for itself as a presence to itself.

Second movement is that of selfness when possible is reflected on the consciousness and determines it as what it is. Possible is to the for-itself as reflection to reflecting but that it is absent-presence.

The free relation of for-itself to himself is in the form of lack which constitutes selfness and for-itself in form of itself is beyond grasp in form of possibilities. Here the 'circuit of selfness' is more clear as it relates to that totality of beings of the world which are within our possibilities. Sartre takes Heidegger's definition that the world is 'that in terms of which human reality makes known to itself what it is.'

Thus the world by nature is mine in so far as it is the correlative in-itself of nothingness. Without world there is no selfness, no person; without selfness, without the person, there is no world. Now Sartre return to the 'I' of Ego saying that person's belonging to the world is never on pre-reflective Cogito, this is a structure which 'I' live. The world is mine because haunted by my possible. It is these possible which give the world its unity and its meaning as a world.

Temporality

Structure of nothingness explains that the human reality is temporal and meaning of its transcendence lies in its temporality. Temporality is an organized structure of three 'elements' –the past, the present and the future.

> *The three so called elements of past, present and future, should not be considered as a collection of 'givens' for us to sum up-for example as an infinite series of nows' in which some are not yet and others are no longer, but rather as the structured moments of an original synthesis.*[97]

Sartre suggest study of temporality in totality as it can solve the problem of understanding three dimensions of time properly as it is totality which confers on them their meaning.

Phenomenology of the Three Temporal Dimensions

Sartre explains phenomenological concept of the three temporal ekstases as follows:

The Past: Every theory about memory implies the presupposition of the being of the past. Sartre explains that, as present is presence in the world, the problem of the past can be solved as its being an intra-mundane being. The being of intra mundane instant is, 'being is', which is entire positivity. This 'being' has nothing to do with 'what is not' and with 'what is no longer'. No negation lies in this density of 'being', hence we see that bridges to past are cut. But one way to connect the past to the present is to consider the temporal phenomenon in its totality. Thus Sartre explains the past:

> *My past is first of all mine, that is, that it exists as the function of a certain being which I am. The*

> *past is not nothing; neither is it the present, but at its very source it is bound to a certain present and to a certain future, to both of which it belongs 'myness' relates the past to the present. My past never appears isolated in its 'pastners' it would be absurd even to imagine that it can exist as such. It is originally the past of this present.*[98]

Sartre explains that my past of yesterday exists as a transcendence behind my present of today. He takes an example of Paul, once who was a student at the polytechnic, the same Paul is thirty years old at present. Being a student is the past of the present Paul. Thus past is characterized as a past of something or of somebody; one has a past, it is this instrument, this society, this man who has a past. There is not first a universal past which would later be particularized in concrete past, on the contrary, it is particular past which we discover first.

The past Sartre is talking about is that of a living person but the past of a dead person has been dealt in the different manner by him. If a person is now dead, we recall him, about his habits, and with the acts he had performed in the past and all the memories about the dead person we have in our minds. Existence of dead person has formed a past of a present, for me and for-others. So past of a dead person cannot exist for him but it is for others.

Sartre says that our past is related to the future through possibilities. Our future possibilities are concrete possibilities, which we have to be and past possibilities are consumed possibilities. The meaning of the past can be changed if it is connected through the present to the future. It means that the project which has roots in the past, is to be actualized in the future. But content of the past cannot be changed, and we can say that past is what it is, it is an in-itself like the things of the world.

> *Whatever I can be said to be in the sense of being-in-itself with a full, compact density (he is quick-tempered, he is a civil servant, he is dissatisfied) is always my past. It is in the past that I am what I am.*[99]

For-itself as its own foundation tries to make itself free from the past which is the in-itself but it never succeeds. The surpassed in-itself lives on and haunts the for-itself as its original contingency.

> *'Facticity' and 'Past' are two words to indicate one and the same thing. The past, in fact, like facticity is the invulnerable contingency of the in-itself which I have to be, without any possibility of not being it. It is the inevitability of the necessity of fact, not by virtue of necessity but by virtue of fact. It is the being of fact, which cannot determine the content of my motivations but which paralyzes them with its contingency because they can neither suppress it nor change it.*[100]

The Present: Present is the for-itself right now. What exists in the present is distinguished from all other existence by the characteristics of presence. The Present is opposed to absent as well as to the past. This meaning of the present is 'presence to'. 'Present to' is an internal relation between the being which is present and the being to which it is present. Anything which can be present to must be such in its being that there is in it a relation of being with other beings. A being which is present to; cannot be at rest as 'in-itself'; the in-itself cannot be present any more than it can be past. The present therefore can be only the presence of the for-itself to being-in-itself.

But the for-itself makes itself presence to being by making itself to be the for-itself and it ceases to be presence by ceasing to be the for-itself. The for-itself is defined as presence to being.

> *The for-itself is presence to all of being-in-itself. Or rather the presence of the for-itself is what makes being-in-itself exist as a totality. Beings are revealed in the world where the for-itself unites them with its own blood by that total ecstatic sacrifice of the self which is called presence.*[101]

Present to a being implies that one is bound to that being by an internal bond, but this is a negative bond. Ontological structure of the for-itself makes it clear that the for-itself is related to the in-itself through negation. the for-itself is present to being in the form of flight, in the form of escape. Thus the fundamental meaning of the present is revealed as the present is not. The present instant emanates from the realistic and reifying conception of the for-itself. Present mode of the for-itself is the same to which it is present. But we cannot say that the present can be grasped in the instant. On the other hand the for-itself is continuously in the making process, it makes itself in the form of flight. We can just say that the instant would be the moment when the present is.

> *As being for-itself it has its being outside of it before and behind. Behind it was past; and before it will be its future. It is a flight outside of co-present being and from the being which it was toward the being which it will be. At present it is not what it is (Past) and it is what it is not (Future).*[102]

The Future: Sartre explains that the in-itself can be neither a future nor contains a past of the future. It is only by human reality that the future arrives in the world. If the future is pre-outlined on the horizon of the world, this can be only by a being which is its own future. Only a being which has to be its being instead of simply being it can have a future. We can understand the relation of the future to the for-itself as its own future on the basis of original and prejudicative relation of itself to itself. It is the being which comes to itself in terms of the future, the being which makes itself exist as having its being outside itself in the future.

> *There is in my consciousness no moment which is not similarly defined by an internal relation to a future when I write, when I smoke, when I drink, when I rest, the meaning of my conscious states is always at a distance, down there, outside.*[103]

He says that the future is what I have to be, in so far as I cannot be it. The for-itself makes itself present before being as not being this being. This Presence is flight an escape of being toward. The possible is that which the for-itself lacks in order to be itself or, the appearance of what I am-at a distance. Thus we grasp the meaning of the flight which is presence; it is a flight towards its being; that is toward the self which it will be by coincidence with what it lacks. The future is the lack which wrenches it as a lack, away from the in-itself of presence.

The future is the determining being which the for-itself has to be beyond being. There is a future because the for-itself has to be its being instead of simply being it. Future being is in the mode of not yet, as a nothingness, its complement of being is at a distance from itself, means it's a beyond being. But we cannot say that future is not solely the presence of the for-itself to a being situated beyond being. It is something which waits for the for-itself that is I. This something is myself.

If I say "I will be happy," it combines the three elements of temporality i.e. the past, the present and the future. Here 'I' the present is dragging the past after it, who will be happy in future. Thus future is I in as much as I await myself as presence to a being beyond being. I project myself towards the future in order to merge there with that which I lack.

The future is the ideal point where the sudden infinite compression of facticity (past), of the for-itself (present), and of its possible (a particular future) will at last cause the self to arise as the existence in-itself of the For-itself. The project of the for-itself towards the future which it is a project towards the in-itself.

> *It is the very nature of the For-itself that it must be 'an always future hollow It slides into the past as a bygone future, and the present For-itself in all its facticity is revealed as the foundation of its own nothingness and once again as the lack of a new future.*[104]

Sartre explains with an example that, my final position on the ground of the tennis court has determined on the ground of the future all my intermediary positions, and finally it has been reunited with an ultimate position identical with what it was in the future as the meaning of my movements.

The future is strictly opposed to the Past. Past is in-itself with no possibility of change in its content. This is what has been defined as being it past behind itself. Being of the future is that I can only be it. My freedom gnaws at its being from below. Thus the future is meaning of my present as its own possibility. But this is not fixed future giving way to a sort of determinism but as for-itself is foundation of its nothingness, the future can effect only pre-outline of the limits within which the for-itself will make itself be as a flight making itself present to being in the direction of another future.

The for-itself is free, and its freedom is to itself its own limit. future qua future does not have to be. It is not the in-itself and neither is it in the mode of being of the for-itself since it is the meaning of for-itself. The future is not, it is possibilized.

The Ontology of Temporality

The ontology of temporality means the structural point of view and in this regard it is related to the ontological structure of the for-itself. Sartre says that:

> *Temporality is not a universal time containing all being and in particular human realities. Neither is it a law of development which is imposed on being from without, nor is it being. But it is the intra-structure of being which is its own nihilation, that is the mode of being peculiar to being-for-itself. The for-itself is the being which has to be its being in the diasporatic form of temporality.*[105]

First of all Sartre explains the basic theme of time which explains before-after in ontological terms. Its meaning is simple. Before-after is defined first of all by irreversibility. We call it successive as we can consider the terms only one at a time and only in one direction. Some times it is taken as separation actually time does separate me from the realization of my desires. If I am obliged to wait for that realization, it is because it is located after other events. Without this 'after' there would be no distance between the present me and later me.

> *Time separates me from myself, from what I have been, from what I wish to be, from what I wish to do, from things, and from others. This town is half hour away, it will take three days to finish the work etc. It results from these premises that a temporal vision of the world and of man will dissolve into a crumbling of before and afters.*[106]

Only a being of a certain structure of being can be temporal in the unity of its being. Temporality must have a structure of selfness. Temporality exists only as the intra-structure of a being which has to be its own being;

that is, as the intra-structure of a for-itself. Temporality is not, but the for-itself temporalizes itself by existing. The for-itself cannot be except in the temporal form.

It is through human reality that multiplicity comes into the world; it is the quasi-multiplicity at the heart of being-for-itself which causes number to be revealed in the world. Here multiplicities mean various relations to its being. A for-itself has three ecstatic dimensions. Meaning of ekstasis is distance from self. It is impossible for a consciousness not to exist in there three dimensions.

The Past: The first dimension is past. It is surpassed facticity. The past is a necessary structure of the for-itself; for the for-itself can exist only as a nihilating surpassing and this surpassing implies something surpassed. There is no absolute beginning which without ever having a past would become past. Since the for-itself qua for-itself has to be its past, it comes into the world in the ecstatic unity of a relation with its past.

Problem of Birth—As the past is always there in the ontological structure of the for-itself, the problem of birth is important from this point of view as how can we determine the past before birth. Sartre says that there is no absolute beginning which without ever having a past would become past. So the for-itself comes into the world with a past. Now the question arises that, how can there be past at a time of birth? Sartre explains that:

> *It seems shocking that consciousness 'appears' at a certain moment, that it comes 'to inhabit' the embryo, in short that there is a moment when the living being in the formation is without consciousness and a moment when a consciousness without a past is imprisoned in it. But shock will cease if it appears that there can be no consciousness without a past. The relation of the present for-itself to the for-itself become in-*

> *itself, hides from us the primitive relation of pastness, which is a relation between the for-itself and the pure In-itself. In fact it is as the nihilation of the In-itself that the for-itself arises in the world and it is by this absolute event that the past as such is constituted as the original, nihilating relation between the For-itself and in-itself.*[107]

Thus originally the for-itself is related to a being which is not consciousness. This explanation which gives ontological meaning to the problems of birth according to Sartre is theoretically true but as there is factual limit of memory it cannot be understood practically.

The Present: Second dimension is called the Present. It is nihilation, the for-itself apprehends itself as a certain lack. It is this lack and it is also the lacking. In this not-yet, the nihilating freedom is exercised. Here the for-itself is at a distance from itself. The for-itself is before itself, behind itself: never itself. This is the very meaning of the two ekstatses Past and Future.

The Future: As far as third dimension is concerned we cannot get a hold on being. The for-itself is dispersed in the game of reflected-reflecting. Here being is everywhere and nowhere. When one tries to seize it, it is there before one, it has escaped.

The present, the past and the future, all at the same time, the for-itself dispersing its being in three dimensions is temporal due to the very fact that it nihilates itself. No one of these dimensions has any ontological priority over the other, none of them can exist without the other two.

> *Present is not ontologically prior to the past and to the future: it is conditioned by them as much as it conditions them. But it is the mould of*

> *indispensable non-being for the total synthetic forms of Temporality.*[108]

The Dynamic of Temporality

Dynamics means related to the movement. Thus he says that:

> *Without change there is no temporality since time could not get any hold on the permanent and the identical.*[109]

Transcendence

The for-itself and the in-itself are two parts of a being which by nature are isolated beings in their regions but their relation makes the world. Although at first glance it seems inconceivable but Sartre explains that, relation between them is a primitive upsurge and it forms a part of the very structure of these beings. The concrete is revealed to us as the synthetic totality of which is consciousness, like the phenomenon, constitutes only the articulations. Here key to the relation is not in-itself but for-itself, we call it knowing. Thus consciousness is defined as:

> *A being such that in its being, its being is in question in so far as this being implies a being other than itself.*[110]

Now the question is, if in-itself is what it is, how and why the being of the for-itself have to be a knowledge of the in-itself? And what is general is knowledge? The answer is to be found in the very being of the for-itself. This answer lies hidden in the very meaning of for- itself and in-itself, .for itself has no meaning in isolation as consciousness is consciousness with relation to other and in it-self also does not exist alone i.e. without being appearing to consciousness.

Knowledge

Sartre concludes this discussion about the for-itself, saying that being of the for-itself is knowledge of being and the knowledge has being also. The world is human and the consciousness has particular position. Being is everywhere, it weighs down on me, and it besieges me. I am referred from being to being. If I want to grasp it I find nothing but myself. This is because knowledge intermediate between being and non-being refers me to the absolute Being. Knowledge puts us in the presence of the absolute and there is a truth of knowledge. But this truth, although releasing to us nothing more and nothing less than the absolute, remains strictly human.

The Existence of Others

Sartre's description of the for-itself explains that its ontological structure is subjective experience. But Sartre explains one more mode of consciousness within reflective description, when the for-itself remaining strictly for-itself, points to a radically different type of ontological structure which makes it realize its objectivity. This ontological structure is denoted with the word mine. This structure is realized by the for-itself when he feels presence of the other for-itself. This structure shows that the for-itself is being noticed by the other and the for-itself can never know this image which the other has in his mind about this for-itself.

> *It is in relation to myself as subject that I am concerned about myself, and yet this concern (for-myself) reveals to me a being which is my being without being-for-me.*[111]

Sartre describes the 'Others' using an example of 'shame' and explains how Others appear on the scene. Shame is non-positional, self-consciousness, conscious of itself as shame but It is accessible to reflection. Its structure is intentional as it is a shameful apprehension of something and this something is me. It would be like, "I am ashamed of myself", therefore realization of intimate relation of myself to myself. Although it is non-positional, some aspects of the shame are to be discovered through reflection. Shame means always shame before somebody. It denotes presence of the other, as though an awkward gesture or something vulgar which primarily was just an expression in the mode of non-positional consciousness, I come to realize that there is someone who is there to judge me, to watch me; I become conscious of myself and feel ashamed of vulgarity of my gesture. The reflection which my consciousness is going through at the moment belongs to myself and the Other becomes a mediator between me and myself.

> *I am ashamed of myself as I appear to the Other. By mere appearance of the Other, I am put in the position of passing judgment on myself as an object, for it is as an object that I appear to the Other.*[112]

Shame is by nature recognition. I recognize that I am as the Other sees me. There is however no question of comparison between what I am for myself and what I am for the other. The comparison is impossible; I am unable to bring about any relation between what I am in the intimacy of the for-itself, without distance, without recoil, without perspective, and this and this unjustifiable being-in-itself which I am for the other. Shame is shame of oneself before the other. There are a lot more structures of my being which can be realized fully in the presence of the other. For-itself refers to the for-other. Now the question is, how do we realize the existence of others. Whether it is through body, expressions, soul, gestures, act, conduct etc. It's a complicated problem.

> *At the origin of the problem of the existence of others, there is a fundamental presupposition: others are the other, that is the self which is not myself. Therefore we grasp here a negation as the constitutive structure of the being-of-others. The presupposition common to both idealism and realism is that the constituting negation is an external negation. The other is the one who is not me and the one who I am not. This does not indicate nothingness as a given element of separation between the other and myself. Between the other and myself there is a nothingness of separation. This nothingness does not derive its origin from myself nor from the other, nor it a reciprocal relation between the other and myself. On the contrary, as a primary absence of relation, it is originally the foundation of all relation between the other and me.*[113]

According to Sartre the other appears to me empirically through the perception of a body and this body is an in-itself external to my body. So this relation which unites and separates our bodies is spatial relation, the relation of things which have no relation among themselves. Sartre gives four observations about the existence of the other: These are called proofs by Sartre:

1. The first proof says that it common sense observation of the existence of the others. He says that actually I have always known that I existed, and this is known in the self-consciousness, the same way I have always known that the other existed, that I have always had a total comprehension of his existence, that this 'pre-ontological' comprehension comprises a surer and deeper understanding of the nature of the other and the relation of his being to my being than all the theories which have been built around it.

2. The second proof says that it is again through the cogito, that I examine the outside world and my consciousness throws me onto the other, just as it threw me outside upon the in-itself; and this must be done by disclosing to me the concrete, indubitable presence of a particular, concrete other, just it has already revealed to me my own incomparable, contingent but necessary and concrete existence. Here Sartre just talks about contingent existence of objects and the other people, as he himself is a contingent existence.
3. The third proof says that the other is neither a representation nor a system of representations nor a necessary unity of our representations, he cannot be probable: he cannot at first be an object. Therefore if he is for us, this can be neither as a constitutive factor of our knowledge of the world nor as a constitutive factor of our knowledge of the self, but as one who 'interests' our being and that not as he contributes a priori to constitute our being but as he interests it concretely and 'ontically' in the empirical circumstances of our facticity.
4. Finally he says that no abstract concept of consciousness can result from the comparison of my being-for-myself with my object state for the other. Furthermore this totality like that of the for-itself-is a detotalized totality; for since existence-for-others is a radical refusal of the other, no totalitarian and unifying synthesis of Others is possible.

The Look

How the for-itself recognizes the other for-itself is explained by Sartre through the description of the Look of the other. As subjectivity of the for-itself says that one for-itself can never know the other for-itself in his subjectivity, because it is not possible for anyone to come out of one;s subjectivity. Thus Sartre explains the other through his look. He says that the ordinary appearance of the other in the field of my perception is the main thing which is going to establish the fundamental relation between me and the other. The appearance must be capable of revealing to us, at least as a reality aimed at, the relation to which it refers.

> *Now this appearance is this, "woman I see coming towards me, this man who is passing by in the street, this beggar whom I hear calling before my window, etc. are all for me objects; like other objects of the world and reveal facticity of the world to me and I in my consciousness know myself as an subject". But if this objectness of the other is treated as a fundamental relation between us, existence of the other becomes conjectural. It leads to probability and probability say that this man is man or a perfected robot, the voice of man I hear is of him or a sound from musical instrument; thus probability takes us to the aim of our observation so without going beyond the limits of probability and indeed because of this probability, my apprehension of the other as an object essentially refers me to a fundamental apprehension of the other in which he will not be revealed to me as an object but as a "presence in person".*[114]

It is in the reality of everyday life that the other appears to us, and his probability refers to everyday reality. We take an example; A man is sitting in the lawn on a bench. There is distance between me and the lawn, between me and that man, between that man and other objects of the lawn. These distances giving a character of negation draw out the meanings which remain on the ground of probability. May this object is a man. If I give it to the real that it is a man, then the fact that he is seeing the lawn becomes probable as may be he is thinking something else, may be he is blind etc. All the things appear me through a single look as a totality, at a single stroke of a moment.

Now one more relation appears. Relation of man as an object, to the lawn which is an object. That man being the fundamental term of the relations, the whole thing escapes me and I cannot put myself now at the center of it. The distance appears as a disintegration of the relations which I apprehend between the objects of my universe. Thus the appearance among the objects of my universe of disintegration in that universe is what I mean by the appearance of a man in my universe.

A space which is grouped around the other is, and this space is made with my space there is a regrouping in which I take part but which escapes me, a regrouping of all the objects which people my universe.

> *Suddenly an object has appeared which has stolen the world from me. Everything is in place; everything still exists for me; but everything is traversed by an invisible flight and fixed in the direction of a new object. The appearance of the other in the world corresponds therefore to a fixed sliding of the whole universe, to a decentralization of the world which undermines the centralization which I am simultaneously effecting." But the other is still an object for me. Rather it appears that the world has a kind of drain hole in the middle of its being and that it is perpetually flowing off through this hole.*[115]

Now the important point of inquiry has reached to us. Sartre says that If the other which I perceive as an object, can see what I see then there is recognition of the fact of that other, as; 'other-as-subject'; the same way as in my consciousness I feel my subjectivity. If my look grants me my subjectivity then his look grants him his subjectivity, with my permanent possibility of being seen by the other as an object. For just as the other is a probable object for me – my being a subject; so I can discover myself in the process of becoming a probable object for only a certain subject. I cannot be an object for an object. A radical conversion of the other is necessary if he is to escape objectivity. The look, of the other on me is not from an objective being. The other cannot look at me as he looks at the grass. My objectivity cannot itself derive for me from the objectivity of the world since I am precisely the one by whom there is a world; that is the one who on principle cannot be an object for himself.

> *'Being-seen-by-the-other' is the truth of 'seeing-the-other'. Thus the notion of the other cannot under any circumstances aim at a solitary, extra-mundane consciousness which I cannot even think. The man is defined by his relation to the world and by his relation to myself. He is that object in the world which determines an internal flow of the universe, an internal hemorrhage. My original relation of myself to the other is a concrete, daily relation which at each instant I experience. At each instant the other is looking at me.*[116]

The world with its objects and the other men, as an ensemble exists only in relation to the free projects of my possibilities, this we shall call situation.

> *The situation reflects to me at once both my facticity and freedom; on the occasion of a certain objective structure of the world which surrounds me, it refers my freedom to me in the form of tasks to be freely done. There is no constraint here since my freedom eats into my possible and since correlatively the potentialities of the world indicate and offer only themselves.*[117]

Now we can find out the changes and modification in consciousness when we are in a situation. It means that

I am suddenly affected in my being and that essential modifications in my structure can be apprehended by means of a reflective cogito. First of all I exist for myself as unreflective consciousness. But the for-itself cannot even exist as unreflective consciousness in isolation.

The self which was given in the form of an object, only for reflective consciousness, when for-itself was alone in the capacity of for-itself, it now haunts the unreflective consciousness. Now unreflective consciousness is consciousness of the world and the self exists on the level of objects in the world. Initially the person was an object for consciousness but now, the unreflective consciousness does not apprehend the person directly or as its object; the person is presented to consciousness in so far as the person is an object for the other. I feel my foundation outside myself.

Nevertheless I am that Ego; I do not reject it as a strange image, but it is present to me as a strange image, but it is present to me as a self which I am without knowing it. Shame or pride, as an example, reveals to me the other's look and myself at the end of that look. Now shame reveals to me my self. It is recognition of the fact that I am that object which the other is looking at and judging. My freedom escapes me in order to become a given object. The bond between my unreflective consciousness and my Ego, which is being looked at, is a bond not of knowing but of being.

Thus I am my Ego for the other in the midst of a world which flows towards the other. This way the freedom of the other is revealed to me. Thus the being which I am for the other is not my possible. Yet by shame I claim it as mine, that freedom of another.

> *Shame reveals to me that I am this being, not in the mode of 'was' or of 'having to be' but in-itself. For the other I am seated as this inkwell is on the table; I am leaning over the keyhole as this tree is*

> *bent by the wind. Thus for the other I have stripped myself of transcendence. My original fall is the existence of the other. Shame, like Pride is the apprehension of myself as a nature although that very nature escapes me and is unknowable as such. Strictly speaking it is not that I perceive myself losing my freedom in order to become a thing but my nature is – over there, outside my lived freedom – as a given attribute of this being which I am for the other.*[118]

The conversion of the for-itself into an object not only tries to snatch the freedom but merges him into the world of instrumental complexes. He says that object of the world which have objective, ideal property creating instrumental complexes in the situation are turned towards the other. To apprehend myself as seen is, in fact to apprehend myself as seen in the world and from the standpoint of the world. The look does not carve me out in the universe but it comes to search for me at the heart of my situation and grasps me only in irresolvable relations with instruments.

This situation creates clash among possibilities as possibility of one for-itself may be a hindrance to the other and his may be hindrance to the this particular for-itself. For the other my possibility is an obstacle, for it will compel him to new act. Every act performed against the other can on principle is for the other an instrument which will serve him against him. Sartre says that I am no longer master of the situation. My being an object for the other is called Being-for -others. But this being for others is not an ontological structure of the Being-for-itself.

Our human-reality must of necessity be simultaneously be for-itself and for-others. Although it is possible to conceive of a for-itself wholly free from all for-others and which would exist without even suspecting the possibility of being an object. But this for-itself simply would not be a 'Man'. It is the factual necessity that our being along with its being-for-itself is also being-for-others. The being which is revealed to the reflective consciousness is for-itself-for-others.

> *Yet this limit beyond reach, the self-as-object, is not ideal; it is a real being. This being is not in-itself for it is not produced in the pure exteriority of indifference. But neither is it for-itself, for it is not the being which I have to be by nihilating myself. It is precisely my being-for-others this being which is divided between two negations with opposed origins and opposite meanings. For the other is not this me of which he has an intuition and I do not have the intuition of this Me which I am. Yet this Me, produced by the one and assumed by the other, derives its absolute reality from the fact that it is the only separation possible between two beings fundamentally identical as regards their mode of being and immediately present one to the other; for since consciousness alone can limit consciousness, no other mean is conceivable between them. In view of this presence of the other-as-subject to me in and through my assumed objectness, we can see that my making an object out of the other must be second moment in my relation to him.*[119]

Sartre says that the Other cannot be known in his subjectivity but through the real life circumstances. The difference of principle between the other-as-object and the other-as-subject stems solely from the fact that objects of the world do not refer to his subjectivity: they refer only to his object state in the world as the meaning – surpassed toward my selfness of the intra-mundane flow. Sartre here quotes one example of a man in this regard, reading in a subway;

> *Around this man the entire world is present. It is not his body only, as an object in the world, which defines him in his being; it is his identity card, it is the direction of the particular train which he has boarded, it is the ring which he wears on his finger. Not as a result of the signs of what he is; this notion of a sign, in fact, would refer us to a subjectivity which I cannot even conceive and in which he is precisely nothing, since he is what he is not an is not what he is; but by virtue of real characteristics of his being.*[120]

Thus we cannot reach subjectivity of the other as he is what he is not and is not what he is. One more example shows the importance of this principle of otherness and that is of the dead. A man loses his subjectivity when he is dead so only the dead can be perpetually objects without ever becoming subjects, for to die is not to lose one's objectivity in the midst of the world; all the dead are there in the world around us. But to die is to lose all possibility of revealing oneself as subject to the other.

Being-for-other is third ekstasis of the for-itself. Ekstatis is a greek word used by Sartre to describe the for-itself in its capacity, being separated from the self. Sartre explains the three ekstases as such:

1. Temporality – The for-itself nihilates the In-itself in the three dimensions of past, present and future. [The three temporal ekstatis].
2. Reflection -The for-itself tries to adopt an external point of view on itself.
3. Being-for-others – The for-itself discovers that it has a self for-the-other, a self which it is, without ever being able to know a get hold of it.

Sartre says that the other's existence can be experienced with evidence in and through the fact of my objectivity. My reaction to my own alienation for the other is expressed in my grasping the other as an object. So the other exists in two ways for us.

> *If I experience him with evidence, I fail to know him; if I know him, If I act upon him, I only reach his being-as-object and his probable existence in the midst of the world. No synthesis of these two forms is possible.*[121]

The Body

Sartre's description of the body becomes the most interesting part of his theory as he reverses the old dictum about soul (consciousness) and body. The famous saying is that 'soul individualizes the body' but Sartre explains that body individualizes the for-itself, which is the consciousness. He deals with the concept of body as a concrete presence of the for-itself in the world and utilizes it as a mean of relations with things and other men in the world.

He says that the other is an object for me and I am an object for the other and this is manifested through the body. Body, a living object is composed of nervous system, brain, glands, digestive, respiratory and circulatory organs, which can be analyzed biologically. Its very matter is capable of being analyzed chemically into atoms of hydrogen, carbon, nitrogen, phosphorus etc., it shows its objective nature. But our consciousness is different from our body as it is related to the subjectivity of a man. Thus relation between body and consciousness is obscured by the fact that the one is objective and the other is subjective.

But Sartre says that as all men have same kinds of structure of internal and external body It is most important' to choose the order of bits of our knowledge because the man cannot be defined in the manner of physicians, so far as the physicians have had any experience with my body, it was with my body in the midst of the world and as it is for others. So examination needs to be on different lines. He says that:

> *It was much more my property than my being.*[122]

Nature of the body is to be examined on two ontological levels, Being-for-itself and Being-for-others according to Sartre:

The Body as Being-For-Itself (Facticity):

The for-itself is both body and consciousness. For-itself and the world are not two close entities, but for-itself is a relation to the world. Man and the world are relative beings and the principle of their being is the relation. The first relation proceeds from human-reality to the world. For human-reality, to be is to-be-there: that is "there in that chair", "there at that table", "there at the top of that mountain, with these dimensions, this orientation", etc. All these things denote to the body. It is an ontological necessity. In this sense we could define the body as the contingent form which is assumed by the necessity of its contingency.

> *The body is nothing other than the for-itself; it is not an in-itself in the for-itself, for in that case it would solidify everything. But it is the fact that the for-itself is not its own foundation, and this act is expressed by the necessity of existing as an engaged, contingent being among other contingent beings. As such the body is not distinct from the situation of the for-itself since for the for-itself, to exist and to be situated are one and the same; on the other hand the body is identified with the whole world in as much as the world is the total situation of the for-itself and the measure of its existence.*[123]

Being a situation in the world, body is contingency, it is facticity for the for-itself. Body is the recognition and individualization of the for-itself. Body is the in-itself which is surpassed by the nihilating for-itself and which reapprehends the for-itself in this very surpassing.

Body is a necessary characteristics of the for-itself. The very nature of the for-itself demands that it be a body; that is, that its nihilating escape from being should be made in the form of an engagement in the world. There is no difference between soul and the body in Sartre theory as it is only body which individualizes the for-itself.

How the subjectivity and the objectivity is combined in the body is explained by an example of the scientific experiment, where one subject helps to make one objective theory. He says that sources of perception in the body are sense–organs and experiments are done by physiologists on them. For example, eye; between me and the eye which I dissect there is interposed the whole world such as I make it appear by my very upsurge. The empirical knowledge of the body is sufficient to prove our existence in the world and above that it enables us to reach the inside of the 'other-as-object'. It has been established that through the ensemble of objective establishment in the scientific field, if we act on certain senses we 'provoke a modification' in the other's consciousness.

Now a new question arises. My sensations belongs my subjectivity, the subjectivity which is selfness. All the experiments done in the scientific field are objective and belong to the objectness, which is other in the eyes of the experimenter. If an experiment is done on me, I am an object, as the other in the eyes of the researcher.

> *Therefore the result obtained at the end of the experiment could be only the relating of two series of objects: those which were revealed to me during*

> *the same period to the experimenter. The illumination of the screen belonged to my world; my eyes as objective organs belonged to the world of the experimenter. The connection of these two series was held to be like, a bridge between two worlds, under no circumstances could it be a table of correlation between the subjective and the objective.*[124]

As always I surpass what is revealed to me toward the possibility which I have to be – for example, toward that of replying correctly to the experimenter and of enabling the experiment to succeed. Of course these comparisons give certain objective results.

Subjective is that which cannot get out of itself. The subjective quality of the other-as-object is purely and simply a closed box. Sensation is inside the box. Sensation does not correspond to anything which I experience in myself or with regard to the other.

As man is provided with sense organs and his sensations tell him that he is already in the world. Sensations belong with the lived. It is sensation which I give as a basis of my knowledge of the external world. For example if I see or touch my sense organs, they are revealed to me like objects of the world and not like a revealing or constructive activity. But sight, touch, hearing show that there are senses.

To say that I have entered into the world, 'come to the world' or 'there is a world', or that 'I have a body' is one and the same thing. In this sense my body is co-extensive with the world, spread across all things. All variations which can be registered in a perceptive field are objective variations. In particular the fact that one can cut off vision by 'closing the eye lids' an external fact which does not refer to the subjectivity of apperception. The accidents which affect a sense belong to the province of objects. 'I see yellow' because I have jaundice or because I am wearing yellow glasses. In each case the reason for phenomenon is not found in a subjective modification of the sense nor even in an organic change but in an objective relation between objects in the world; In each case I see 'through' something and the truth of my vision is objective. Finally in one way or another the center of visual reference is destroyed (since destruction can come only from the development of the world according to its own laws – i.e. expressing in a certain way my facticity,) visible object are not by the same stroke annihilated. They continue to exist for me, but they exist without any center of reference, as a visible totality without the appearance of any particular this; that is, they exist in the absolute reciprocity of their relations.

Thus Sartre explains that it is the upsurge of the for-itself in the world which by the same stroke causes the world to exist as the totality of things and causes senses to exist as the objective mode in which the qualities of things are presented. Blindness, myopia, daltonism originally represent the way in which there is a word for me; that is they define my visual sense in so far as this is the facticity of my upsurge.

Whatever is done by the man is through the body only so body is not defined as only 'the seat of five senses' but also the instrument and the end of our actions. Every man's body is an instrument for the other man in the midst of the world.

The for-itself relates to the in-itself through the body. Sartre says that the instrumental things indicate other instruments as objective way of making use of them: the nail is "to be pounded in this way or that, the hammer is to be held by the handle", the cup is "to be picked up by its handle," etc. All these properties of things are immediately revealed. Thus the world appears to me as objectively articulated it never refers to a creative subjectivity but to infinity of instrumental complexes.

> *My body always extends across the tool it utilizes. It is at the end of the cone on which I lean and against the earth: it is at the end of the telescope which shows me the stars; it is on the chair, in the whole house; for it is my adaptation to these tools. Thus sensation and action are rejoined and become one. So we come to the conclusion that the body is as such the original relation to the world for for-itself. In the midst of being the upsurge of body, that is through things of the world, which are instrumental things, the body knows itself. The body is not a screen between things and ourselves; it manifests only individuality and the contingency of our original relation to instrumental things.*[125]

Thus the body in order to define its existence in the midst of the world, acts as Instrumental thing using its senses and sense organs. It is not just to define the individual body but, to define the world also. The body is necessary again, as the obstacle to be surpassed in order to be in the world; that is the obstacle which a man is to himself.It refers to the primary in-itself on the nihilation of which man arises through birth. Thus the body as facticity is the past as it refers originally to birth.

Sartre explains that my birth as it conditions the way in which objects are revealed to me. My race as it is indicated by the other's attitude toward me. My class as it is disclosed by the revelation of the social community to which I belong inasmuch as the places which I frequently refer to it; my nationality; my physiological structure as instruments imply it by the very way in which they are revealed as resistant or docile and by their very coefficient of adversity; my character, my past, as everything which I have experienced is indicated as my point of view on the world by the world itself: all this is so far as I surpass it in the synthetic unity of my being in the world in my body as the necessary condition of the existence of a world and as the contingent realization of this condition.

> *The body is the contingent form which is taken up by the necessity of my contingency. We can never apprehend this contingency as such in so far as our body is for us; for we are a choice, and for us, to be is to choose ourselves. Even the disability from which I suffer I have assumed by the very fact that I live; I surpass it towards my own projects. I make of it the necessary obstacle for my being, and I cannot be crippled without choosing myself as crippled. This means that I choose the way in which I constitute my disability (as 'unbearable', humiliating', 'to be hidden', 'to be revealed to all', 'an object of pride' 'the justification of my failures', etc.). Body conditions consciousness as pure consciousness of the world, it renders consciousness possible even in its very freedom.*[126]

Although body is inapprehensible but our consciousness makes us aware about the body. Body belongs to the non-thetic self-consciousness. Non-thetic self-consciousness being its own nothingness and a possibility towards its free project, it is consciousness of the body as being that which it surmounts and nihilates by making itself consciousness. Consciousness never cease 'to have' a body. Body is pure apprehension of the self as a factual existence.

According to Sartre the feeling of nausea reveals relation of the body to the consciousness, it reveals that how much the efforts be there on the part of consciousness to be relieved from body but body asserts its presence always.

> *This perpetual apprehension on the part of my for-itself of an insipid taste which I cannot place,*

> *which accompanies me every in my effort to get away from it, and which is my taste – this is what put under the name of Nausea. A dull and inescapable Nausea perpetually reveals my body to my consciousness.*[127]

The Body-For-Others:

Sartre says that the other can be known through his body only it says that every for-itself knows the other for-itself as an object and act. He explains it as such:

> *As body is contingency for for-itself, but the body knows the same avatars as the for-itself. Body has other planes of existence; it exists also for-others. The way in which my body appears to the other or the way in which the other's body appears to me amounts to same thing.*[128]

Sartre says that first of all my for-itself apprehends the other as the one for whom I exist as an object; the reapprehension of my selfness then causes the other to appear as an object in the second moment. So the other exists for me first and then I apprehend him in his body subsequently. It's clear that the apprehension of the other's body is not a primary encounter, if I determine my relation with the other.

The body of any for-itself is in the midst of the world being a contingent existence thus body of the other is also contingent and each body serves as an instrument to be utilized with other instruments and is also indicated by the round of instrumental-things.

> *To be sure, the other's body is present everywhere in the very indication which instrumental-things give of it since they are revealed as utilized by him and are known by him. This room in which I wait for the master of the house reveals to me in its totality the body of its owner: this easy chair is a*

> *chair-where he sits, this desk is a desk-at-which-he-writes.*[129]

Although this master is absent but he can fulfill the situation whenever he likes. We cannot discover in and through the other's body the possibility, which the other has of knowing us. This is revealed through my being an object for the other. This is the essential structure of original relation between the for-itself and the other. Apprehending the existence of the other, the selfness which I reapprehend serves to transcend the other's transcendence. The other's transcendence which apprehends me as an object, I surpass it towards my own goals. It is his appearing to me as transcendence – transcended.

Sartre explains that as my own senses are subjective, that of the other also can be assumed to be like that but objectively the senses of the other are known as knowing. The other's sense organs does not necessarily means not any particular face, and finally not this face. But face, sense organs, presence-all that is nothing but the contingent form of the other's necessity to exist himself as belonging to a race, a class and an environment. The flesh is pure contingency of presence. The other's body is then the facticity of transcendence transcended as it refers to my facticity. I apprehend the other's body simultaneously apprehending that of my body. The other's body is always given in a situation or we can say the other's body is that in terms of which there is a situation.

> *The other's body is meaningful; Meaning is nothing other than a fixed movement of transcendence. A body is a body as this mass of flesh which it is defined by the table which the body looks at, the chair in which it sits, the pavement on which it walks, etc. The body is*

> *totality of meaningful relations to the world. In this sense it is defined also by reference to the air which it breathes, to the water which it drinks, to the food which it eats. The body in fact could not appear without sustaining meaningful relations with the totality of what is.*[130]

Sartre says that the flesh is in-itself. So to be in the form of a for-itself, this in-itself is to be suppressed. Biological sciences which deal with flesh or structure of the body understand the man in terms of death and not in terms of life. Its meaning is that living a life is different from being alive. The body of other, which is revealed on biological bases, is erroneous. Even the study of life in the living person, even vivisection, even the study of the life of protoplasm, even embryology or the study of the egg cannot rediscover life; the organ which is observed is living but it is not established in the synthetic unity of the life of a particular person.

> *The other's body is the facticity of the transcendence-transcended as this facticity is perpetually a birth; that is it refers to the indifferent exteriority of an in-itself perpetually surpassed.*[131]

So it is clear that the appearance of the other is transcendence-transcended and body is the facticity of the transcendence-transcended. Body is in space, it is the situation, and in time, it is freedom-as-object. The other's body is always 'a body-more-than-body' because the other is given to the for-self totally and without intermediary in the perpetual surpassing of its facticity. But this surpassing never refers the one to his subjectivity. The other's objectivity is his transcendence as transcended. The body is the facticity of this transcendence. But the other's corporeality and objectivity are strictly inseparable.

The Third Ontological Dimension of the Body:

> *I exist my body: this is its first dimension of being. My body is utilized and known by the other: this is its second dimension. But in so far as I am for others, the other is revealed to me as the subject for whom I am an object. Even there is the question of my fundamental relation with the other. I exist therefore for myself as known by the other – in particular in my very facticity. I exist for myself as a body known by the other. This is the third ontological dimension of my body.*[132]

He says that when the look of the other makes me feel the objective nature of mine which is in the eyes of the other, That in-itself, objective 'Me' is beyond my approach to understand. Because we can never know what is inside or subjectivity of the other. So what the other has point of view of my appearance as in-itself is beyond imagination for me to understand. I feel myself touched by the other in my factual existence. Every for-itself is responsible for this being-there-for-others. This being there is precisely the body thus it makes him feel to be conscious of existing for the other as a flight towards a being-in-the-midst-of-the-world. Sartre says that the other apprehends my body in this encounter as an in-itself, as an instrument. My body escapes me on all sides. My senses which give me all subjective feelings and are even then inapprehensible, seem to be apprehended by the other as in-itself, the same way as I apprehend the senses of the other; biological senses, instrumental senses, working and to be utilized.

> *This instrument which I am is made present to me as an instrument submerged in infinite instrumental series. Although I can in no way view this series by surveying it. My body as alienated escapes me toward a being-a-tool-*

> *among-tools, towards a being-a-sense-organ-apprehended-by-sense-organs, and this is accompanied by an alienating destruction and a concrete collapse of my world which flows toward the other and which the other will reapprehend in the world.*[133]

This third dimension is the realization of alienation of the self. Sartre quotes example of shyness when to feel oneself blushing to feel oneself sweating etc. are expressions, which a shy person uses to describe his body as it is not for him but for the other. This body-for-the-other is in fact body for-us, but inapprehensible and alienated. Sartre says that a child begins the learning process with the other's body, thus the perception of my body is placed chronologically after the perception of the body of the other. Sartre concludes by saying that we should see body as the necessity of a concrete and contingent existence in the midst of the world.

Concrete Relations with The Others

Our fundamental relation with the other first arises in connection with the relation between my body and the other's body. Thus particular relation of my being with that of the other presuppose facticity; that is ever existence as body in the midst of the world.

But concrete relation in the midst of the world show new modes of being on the part of the for-itself. Each relation in its own way presents the bilateral relation : for-itself-for-others, in-itself. It explains all the relations which exist in the world or we can say that there is a relation of the for-itself with the in-itself in the presence of the other.

> *The for-itself as the nihilation of the in-itself temporalizes itself as a flight toward. Actually it*

> *surpasses its facticity (i.e. to be either given or past or body) toward the in-itself which it would be if it were able to be its own foundation. This flight takes place towards an impossible future always pursued where the for-itself would be an in-itself-for-itself. The for-itself is both a flight and a pursuit; it flees the in-itself and at the same pursues it. The for-itself is pursued-pursuing.*[134]

So far it has become clear that the for-itself is the foundation of all negativity and of all relation but the upsurge of the other touches the for-itself in its very heart. The for-itself was escaping the in-itself and character of the for-itself as totality detotalized conferred on it a perpetual 'elsewhere'. Now it is this very totality which the other makes appear before him and which he transcends towards his own 'elsewhere'. This totality is totalized. In this way the particular flight, the particular freedom, which is called subjectivity of the for-itself is now fixed and contemplated in the form of in-itself and this alienation of him happens outside and which cannot be known by him. This results in a decision to assume an attitude with respect to it. Sartre explains it thus:

> *Such is the origin of my concrete relations with the other; they are wholly governed by my attitude with respect to the object which I am for the other. And the other's existence reveals to me the being which I am without my being able either to appropriate that being or even to conceive it.*[135]

So Sartre says that the profound meaning of my being is outside of me. But I can deny this being conferred from outside. I can turn my back upon the other to make an object out of him. As other's objectness destroys my objectness for him. On the other hand as other's freedom is foundation of my being-in-itself. If I identify that freedom, I become my own foundation. Thus two attitudes which can be assumed with respect to other are described by Sartre as such:

> *To transcend the other's transcendence, or, on the contrary, to incorporate that transcendence within me without removing from it its character as transcendence.*[136]

Upsurge of one's being is an upsurge in the presence of the other, to the extent that the one is a pursuing flight and a pursued-pursuing. Every person serves as a proof of the other. This explanation is about the structure of the for-itself, but the presence of the other in the world is absolute and self-evident fact, along with being a contingent fact. And it is impossible to deduce this contingency of the other from the ontological structure of the for-itself. Sartre calls it an organic ensemble of projects towards one's own possibilities. He explains it as an ideal of love as its unique value. When I try to realize this value, I am in direct connection with the other's freedom. So In this sense love is a conflict. Sartre now explains the structure of love as an ideal relation of two selves. He asks the question that why does the lover wants to be loved. If love is a desire for physical possession then it can be easily satisfied. But the total enslavement of beloved kills the love of the lover and the lover finds himself alone. So he wants to possess a freedom as freedom, it means, the lover wants to be loved as a freedom but demands that this freedom as freedom should no longer be free. He wishes that the other's freedom should determine itself to become love. He does not want to act on the other's freedom but to exist a priori as the objective limit of this freedom. To want to be loved is to invest the other with one's own facticity.

What the other conceives in his subjectivity is always unknown as It can be just an assumption and can create fear in a man of being a strange being to himself. Sartre procedes saying that if the other loves me and I become unsurpassable, that means that I must be the absolute end. This way my transcendence is not transcended, I am no longer an instrument in the world and my independence is absolutely safeguarded. Now I am the absolute value. To want to be loved is to want to be placed beyond the whole system of values posited by the other and to be condition of all valorization and the objective foundation of all values.

Before being loved the for-itself considered its existence unjustified, de trop, but after falling in love the existence is willed even in its tiniest details by an absolute freedom. This is basis for the joy of love, when there is joy. We can say that to be in love is to feel that existence is justified.

First Attitude Towards Others

In it Sartre explains the conduct in which the for-itself tries to assimilate the other's freedom. It means that everything which may be said of me in my relations with the other applies to him as well. We are engaged in reciprocal and moving relations.

We know that the conflict is the original meaning of being-for-others. Ontological structure of Being-for-other explains that where as I know my objectness for the other, he is also conscious of it. As Sartre says that "the other holds a secret; the secret of what I am".

Now the attitude with respect to it is that I should be obliged to recover and find, in order to be the foundation of myself. This would be a project of absorbing the other. Since my being-as-object is the only relation between me and the other, this being-as-object will serve me as an instrument to effect my assimilation of the other freedom. To be other to oneself is ideal here which serves as value to this relation. This ideal can be realized by surmounting the original contingency of my relations to the other, but this contingency is insurmountable.

If we think about the relation with point of view of unity, we find that unity with the other is unrealizable. The other is the other because, in my selfness I find that the other is not me. But assimilation of the for-itself and the other, in a single transcendence would necessarily involve the disappearance of the otherness in the other. This project of unification is the source of conflict. As he says:

> *While I experience myself as an object for the other and while I project assimilating him in and by means of this experience, the other apprehends me as an object in the midst of the world and does not project identifying me with himself. It would therefore be necessary – since being-for-others includes a double internal negation-to act upon the internal negation by which the other transcends my transcendence and makes me exist for the other; that is to act upon the other's freedom.*[137]

Sartre explains this attitude through relations of love, language and masochism. The first relation of love is as such:

Love:

Love is a contradictory effort. If the other loves me, he radically deceives me by his very love. I demanded of him that he should found my being as a privileged object by maintaining himself as pure subjectivity confronting me; and as soon as he loves me he experiences me as subject and is swallowed up in his objectivity confronting my subjectivity. The illusion of the game of mirrors which makes the concrete reality of love, suddenly ceases.

Sartre says that the lovers should be looked at together by a third Person in order for each one to experience not only his own objectivation but that of the other as well. Immediately the other is no longer for me the absolute transcendence which founds me in my being; he is a transcendence-transcended, not by me but by another.

> *The triple destructibility of love: in the first place it is, in essence, a deception and a reference to infinity since to love is to wish to be loved, hence to wish that the other wish that I love him. A pre-ontological comprehension of this deception is given in the very impulse of love – hence the lover's perpetual dissatisfaction. It does not come, as is so often said, from the unworthiness of being loved but from an implicit comprehension of the fact that the amorous intuition is, as a fundamental-intuition, an ideal out of reach. The more I am loved, the more I lose my being, the more I am thrown back on my own responsibilities, on my own power to be. In the second place the other's awakening is always possible; at any moment he can make me appear as an object – hence the lover's perpetual insecurity. In the third place love is an absolute which is perpetually made relative by others. One would have to be alone, in the world with the beloved in order for love to preserve its character as an absolute axis of reference – hence the lover's perpetual shame (or pride – which here amounts to be something).*[138]

Language:

All our attempts toward others presuppose language. Language is not a phenomenon added on to being-for-others. It is originally being for others as it is always directed toward the other.

It is clear that subjectivity experiences itself as an object for the other, but language has not been invented between objects, since it presupposes an original relation to another subject. In the inter-subjectivity of the for-others, it is not necessary to invent language because it is given in the recognition of the other. I am language.

Language forms a part of the human condition. It is originally the proof which a for-itself can make of its being-for-others.

Language is not distinct from the recognition of the other's existence. The other's upsurge confronting me as a look makes language arise as the condition of my being. By language Sartre means all the phenomena of expression which are meant for the other, other's freedom gives meaning to them. Thus meaning of my expressions always escapes me. I can only guess at the meaning of what I express, i.e. the meaning of what I am since in this perspective to express and to be are one. The other is always there, present and experienced as the one who gives to language its meaning. Language reveals to the for-itself, freedom (transcendence) of the one who listens to him in silence.

Sartre says that my language is related to me the same way my body is related to me. The problem of language is exactly parallel to the problem of bodies, and the description which is valid in one case is valid in the other

Masochism:

One more attitude which resembles to that of love and that is masochism. It is an attempt not to fascinate the other by means of my objectivity but to cause myself to be fascinated by my objectivity-for-others. But Masochism is a failure as in order to cause myself to be fascinated by my self-as-object, I should have intuitive apprehension of this object such as it is for the other, a thing which on principle is impossible.

The masochist treats the other as an object and transcends him towards his own objectivity, which in spite of himself frees his own subjectivity. Thus masochism is a failure.

Second Attitude towards Others

Sartre explains it saying that In this attitude when the

other has a look on me, means trying to make an object out of me, I assert myself in my freedom confronting the other, I make the other transcendence-transcended-that is an object. 'To look at the look' is the relation of this kind. In my upsurge into the world I build my subjectivity upon the collapse of the subjectivity of the other. The other becomes a being which I possess and which recognizes my freedom. In this way my aim is to transcend his possibilities with all my possibilities. But I feel disappointment when I find that it is not possible to appropriate his freedom as this freedom has collapsed beneath my look. Then next step would be to attempt again to seek other's freedom across the object which he is for me, through appropriation of his body. This is as per principle a failure. Sartre explains different attitudes in this structure. It includes attitudes of indifference, desire sadism and hate.

Indifference:

'To look at the look' is to build my subjectivity upon the collapse of the subjectivity of the other. This attitude we would call Indifference towards others. It's a kind of blindness which I am with regard to others. It includes an implicit comprehension being-for-others; that is of the other's transcendence as a look. This comprehension is simply what I myself determine to hide from myself. Others are forms which pass by in the street, those magic objects which are capable of acting at a distance and upon which I can act by means of determined conduct. I scarcely notice them; I act as if I were alone in the world. I brush against 'people; as I brush against a wall; I avoid them as I avoid obstacles. Their freedom as object is for me only their 'coefficient of adversity'. I do not even imagine that they can look at me. Of course they have some knowledge of me, but this knowledge does not touch me. It is a question of modification of their being which do not pass from them to me and which are tainted with what we call a 'suffered subjectivity' or 'subjectivity as object', that is they express what they are, not what I am, and they are the effect of my action upon them. Sartre describes here people as mere functions: the ticket-collector is only the function of collecting tickets; the café waiter is nothing but the function of serving the patrons. So there is no recognition of them as humans but in this capacity they will be most useful if someone knows their keys and those 'master-words' which can release their mechanisms.

Sartre says that I ignore subjectivity of the other which is foundation of my being-in-itself and my being-for-others, in particular my body-for-others and I try to become sure that the other's look cannot fix my possibilities and my body. We can call it Bad-faith which can last over years and may be for whole life.

But this attitude becomes failure when this blindness toward the other does not release us from the fear of being in danger in other's freedom. It places us at the extreme degree of objectivity at the very moment when we can believe ourselves to be an absolute and unique subjectivity since we are seen without being able to experience the fact that we are seen and without being able by means of the same experience to defend ourselves against our 'being seen'.

Desire:

Sartre expresses desire as a particular mode of subjectivity. Desire is consciousness since it can be only as non-positional consciousness of itself. Desire is not only longing which directs itself through our body toward a certain object but it has been defined by Sartre as trouble also:

> *Our original apprehension of the troubled water is given us as changed by the presence of an invisible something which is not itself distinguished and which is manifested as a pure factual resistance. If the desiring consciousness is*

> *troubled, it is because it is analogous to the troubled water.*[139]

Consciousness chooses itself as desire, and nihilates itself in the upsurge. All the three temporal ekstases find its meaning in desire. The ontological structure of desire is expressed being similar to the process of caress by Sartre, as thought is expressed by language. Here caress means internal modification of the body in desire. Desire residing in the consciousness makes the body present in the world with certain physical features so Sartre calls this process the incarnation.. He gives example of hunger in this regard. As when we are hungry we feel impoverishment of the blood, abundant salivary secretion etc. Sartre calls them facticity. The for-itself becomes conscious of it non-thetically and conscious of it as surpassed facticity. In this way the world appears to the for-itself as a world of desire.

> *Objects then become the transcendent ensemble which reveals my incarnation to me. A contact with them is caress – but to conceive an object when I am in the desiring attitude is to caress myself with it. Thus I am sensitive not so much to the form of the object and to its instrumentality, as to its matter (gritty, smooth, tepid, greasy, rough etc.). In my desiring perception I discover something like a flesh of objects. My shirt rubs against my skin, and I feel it. What is ordinarily for me an object most remote becomes the immediately sensible; the warmth of air, the breath of the wind, the rays of sunshine etc., all are present to me in a certain way, as posited upon me without distance and revealing my flesh by means of their flesh. From this point of view desire is not only the clogging of a consciousness by its facticity. It is correlatively the ensnarement of a*

> *body by the world. The world is made ensnaring; consciousness is engulfed in a body, which is engulfed in the world.*[140]

The important explanation here is that Sartre relates this desire not to the in-itself but to the concrete relations with the other, as the world appears only as the ground for explicit relations with the other. Usually it is on the occasion of the other's presence that the world is revealed as the world of desire. Desire is related to the body of the other as well. Sartre calls it the impossible ideal of desire such as to possess the other's transcendence as pure transcendence and at the same time as body. It is to reduce the other, simply to the facticity, to bring it about that this facticity is a perpetual apprehension of his nihilating transcendence.

Sadism:

Sadism is like desire but it's not wholly desire. In this attitude the person is engaged without any understanding of value. He experiences himself in the face of the other as pure transcendence. Sadism is instrumental appropriation of the other, taking him as the object-as-object, as a pure incarnated transcendence. But it is refusal to be incarnated. But incarnation of the other is through violence and not by caressing. Sartre makes a distinction between love and Sadism.

> *Love does not demand the abolition of the other's freedom but rather his enslavement as freedom, that is, freedom's self-enslavement. Similarly the Sadist does not seek to suppress the freedom of the one whom he tortures but to force his freedom freely to identify itself with the tortured flesh. That is why the moment of pleasure for the torturer is that in which the victim betrays or humiliates himself.*[141]

Sadism is as a seed in desire itself, as the failure of desire.

The explosion of the other's look in the world of the Sadist causes the meaning and goal of sadism to collapse. The sadist discovers that it was that freedom which he wished to enslave and at the same time he realizes the futility of his efforts.

Sartre concludes his description of concrete relations with the other so far saying that all the above explained attitude demonstrate the circle of relations with the other because these attitudes involve in their circularity the integrity of all the conducts towards the other.

> *All the patterns of conduct towards the other-as-object include within themselves as implicit and veiled reference to an other-as-subject, and this reference is their death. Upon the death of a particular conduct toward the other-as-object arise a new attitude which aims at getting hold of the other-as-subject, and this in turn reveals its instability and collapses to give way to the opposite conduct. Thus we are indefinitely referred from the other-as-object to the other-as-subject and vice-versa. The movement is never arrested and this movement with its abrupt reversals of direction constitutes our relation with the other. At whatever moment a person is considered, he is in one or the other of these attitudes – unsatisfied by the one as by the other. We can maintain ourselves for a greater or less length of time in the attitude adopted depending on our bad faith or depending on the particular circumstances of our history. But never will either attitude be sufficient in itself; it always points obscurely in the direction of its opposite. This means that we can never hold a consistent attitude towards the other unless he is simultaneously revealed to us as subject and as object, as transcendence-transcending and as transcendence-transcended,*

> *which is on principle impossible. Thus ceaselessly tossed from being-a-look to being-looked-at, falling from one to the other in alternate revolutions, we are always, no matter what attitude is adopted, in a state of instability in relation to the other. We pursue the impossible ideal of the simultaneous apprehension of his freedom and of his objectivity.*[142]

The other is on principle inapprehensible: he flees me, when I seek him and possesses me when I flee him we are thrown in the world in the face of the other. Our upsurge is a free limitation of his freedom and nothing-not even suicide – can change this original situation I am de trop in relation to others.

Hate:

Futility of all previous attempts about others, in the experience of for-itself of its various avatars, results in death of the other for-itself. This free determination is hate. It implies a fundamental resignation. Hate is an attitude when for-itself abandons its claim to realize any union with the other. It is realization of the world in which the other does not exist. It gives up using the other as an instrument to recover its own being-in-itself, It wishes simply to recover a freedom without factual limits.

> *The one who hates projects no longer being an object; hate presents itself as an absolute positing of the freedom of the for-itself before the other. This is why hate does not abase the hated object, for it places the dispute on its true level. What I hate in the other is not this appearance, this fault, this particular action. What I hate in his existence in general as a transcendence-transcended. This is why hate implies a recognition of the other's freedom. But this recognition is abstract and negative; hate knows only the other-as-object and*

> *attaches itself to his object. It wishes to destroy this object in order by the same stroke to overcome the transcendence which haunts it.*[143]

There is difference between hating and despising. Hate does not necessarily appear on the occasion of one's being subjected to something evil. On the contrary, it can arise when one expects gratitude that is on the occasion of a kindness. The reason behind it is simple as Sartre states that:

> *The occasion which arouses hate is simply an act by the other which puts me in the state of being subject to his freedom. This act is in itself humiliating; it is humiliating as the concrete revelation of my instrumental objectness in the face of the other's freedom.*[144]

Hate aims at the suppression of the other. Hate demands to be hated so that to hate is equivalent to an uneasy recognition of the freedom of the one who hates. Hate is a failure as If the abolition of the other is to be lived as the triumph of hate; it implies the explicit recognition that the other has existed. One cannot free oneself from it. Failure of this attempt is the attempt of despair.

For-itself re-enter the circle and allow itself to be indefinitely tossed from one to the other of the two fundamental attitudes.

Being-with (Mitsein) And the We

Sartre expressed prior relations as the individual ones but in this section he is up to explain relations among a lot of people together. He says that there are certain concrete experiences in which we cannot discover any conflict but community with the other. 'We' is the word we use frequently in this manner. Yet it is nonetheless true that the 'We' subject does not appear even conceivable unless it refers at least to the thought of a plurality of subjects which would simultaneously apprehend one another as subjectivities, that is, as transcendences-transcending and not as a transcendence-transcended.

> *'We' resist, 'We' advance to the attack, 'We' condemn the guilty, 'We' look at this or that spectacle. Thus the recognition of subjectivities is analogous to that of the self-recognition of the non-thetic consciousness.*[145]

There are two radically different forms of experience of the 'We' and the two forms corresponds exactly to the being-in-the-act-of-looking and the being-looked-at which constitute the fundamental relations of the for-itself with the other for-itself. It includes two types of relations: the us-object and the we-subject.

The Us Object

The Us-object precipitates 'us' into the world; we experience it in shame as community alienation. Sartre explains it with an example saying that suppose I am alone with the other in a situation where we are in relation to each other, confronting each other. This situation has objective existence for the one or the other. But actually both of us are related to all others also, that is quasi-totality of consciousness. The other is looking at me and I feel alienated. Now the third person appears on the scene. Here Sartre presents following illustration about possible relations:

1. If the third looks at me then my alienation is not strengthening but I assure them in the category of 'they' through my alienation.
2. But if the third looks at the other the position becomes different. The terms which is revealed in the situation

is other-looked at (by the third). Thus the third transcendence transcends the transcendence which transcends me and thereby contributes to disarming it.

3. If I ally myself to the third so as to look at the other, the other is transformed into an object and 'I and the third' experience the we-as-subject.
4. I look at the third who is looking at the other and I transcends the transcendence of the third which transcends the transcendence of the other. The other transcends my transcendence. The third becomes an object for me, the other an object for the third and I an object for the other. This situation is indeterminate and inconclusive. Here freedom supports itself on one or the other side of relation.
5. I am looking at the other, the third is looking at the other and I am looking at the third also, when he is looking at the other. The third transcends the transcendence of the other making him an object which becomes obvious from the behaviour of the other. The other now flees away from my world and no longer belongs to me. He escapes me not by means of his own transcendence but through the transcendence of the third. The third can be himself looked at by other thirds; that is, can be indefinitely the other whom I do not see. It results in an original instability in the other as an object and an infinite pursuit by the for-itself which seeks to reappropriate this object-state.
6. When I am looking at the other, I experience myself as looked-at by the third. My alienation through the look of the third happens at the same time when I posit the alienation of the other. My transcendence which is ready to transcend the transcendence of the other to make him instrument for my possibilities, falls back to be transcended by the third making my possibilities as dead possibilities and I feel myself unable to make the other as object. This does not mean that the other becomes the subject but he becomes neutral.

Thus Sartre says that I am engaged in a conflict with the other. The third comes on the scène and embraces both of us with his look. I experience my alienation and objectness. For the other I become an object in the midst of a world which is not mine. The other is an object in the midst of the world of the third. Now the object state of mine and that of the other are not parallel, but we find ourselves in the same situation with the appearance of the third. Instrumentality of that of mine and that of the other loses it's in our dead-possibilities. The situation now flees outside my world and the other's world in the objective form in the midst of the third world.

Conflict does not arise, in this objective situation, from the free upsurge of our transcendences, but it is established and transcended by the third as a factual given which defines us and holds us together. I experience it non-thetically, without having knowledge of it. It is free recognition of my responsibility as including the responsibility of the other which is the proof of the us-Object.

> *The Us-object is revealed to us only by my assuming the responsibility for this situation; that is, because of the internal reciprocity of the situation, I must of necessity – in the heart of my free assumption assume also the other.*[146]

Here reciprocity is same as equality, appearance of the third makes me and the other on the same levels making our possibilities as dead possibilities. Neither I, nor the other has upper hand. I cannot say I am fighting but we say, 'we are fighting each other'. 'Us' itself includes the reciprocity, relation on the same plane. The object means both of us in the eyes of the other, who constitutes us as them. This them is assumed by a subjectivity as its meaning for-others becomes 'Us'. Thus is the relation, 'The Us-Object'.

> *It is experienced and which aims at including my belonging as an object to the human totality which is equally apprehended as an object. Therefore it corresponds to an experience of humiliation and impotence; the one who experiences himself as constituting an us with other men feels himself trapped among an infinity of strange existences; he is alienated radically and without recourse.*[147]

There are special forms of the 'Us' in particular to that which we call 'class consciousness'. It is evidently assuming of a particular 'Us' on the occasion of a collective situation more plainly structured than usual.

> *The 'master', the 'feudal lord', the 'bourgeois', the 'capitalist' all appear not only as powerful people who command but in addition and above all Thirds; that is, as those who are outside the oppressed community and for whom this community exists.*[148]

This structure of the us-object collapses when a for-itself looks at the third in turn and reclaims its selfness.

The We-Subject

The 'Us' in class consciousness no longer implies the project of freeing oneself from the 'Us' by an individual recovery of selfness but rather the project of freeing the whole 'Us' from the object state by transforming it into a 'We-subject'.

> *The fact that I am engaged with others in a common rhythm which I contribute to creating is especially likely to lead me to apprehend myself as engaged in a We-subject.*[149]

This rhythm which emanates from me, is my free venture, my transcendence. It synthesizes a future with a present and a past within a perspective of regular repetition. It is I, the for-itself who produce this rhythm. It gets its meaning when it melts into the general rhythm of the work of a concrete community which surrounds me.

The experience of the we-subject is a pure psychological subjective event in a single consciousness. It is modification of the consciousness and not an ontological relation with others. It's a way of feeling myself in the midst of others. According to Sartre the the ideal 'we-subject' would be the 'we' of a humanity which would make itself master of the earth. I apprehend existence of the other on the basis of their factual existence in the world and of the perception of their acts. When we form part of the we-subject, it is non-positional apprehension of the other's body as correlative with my body, of their acts as unfolding in connection with my acts in such a way that I cannot determine whether their acts give birth to my acts or my acts give birth to their acts. Sartre assimilates all kind of relations saying that:

> *It appears that the experience of the 'we' and the 'us', although real is not of a nature to modify the result of prior investigations. As for us-object it is directly dependent on the third and for we-subject this is a psychological experience, which supposes that the existence of the other is already revealed to us. It is therefore useless for human reality to seek to get out of this dilemma: One must either transcend the other or allow oneself to be transcended by him. The essence of the relations between consciousness is not Mitsein; it is conflict.*[150]

Conclusion

The human reality with a point of view of the for-itself is subjectivity while with the point of view of for-others is objectivity. Sartre explains the relation between them through bodies, but it called fundamental relation. In actual sense the concrete relations has been defined on the basic values of love and hate. They serve as balancing poles and all the remaining relations waver between them. Love is a relation dependin on freedom of the other while hate is failure of love. On the whole this chapter deals with the structure of human reality in the world.

Chapter-3
Freedom of Man

Freedom

Sartre has established so far that man is first of all existence and then anything can happen to him. He says that there is no human nature as there is no God to have a conception of it. Man simply is.

> *Everything is indeed permitted if God does not exist, and man is in consequence forlorn...He discovers forthwith that he is without excuse. For if indeed existence precedes essence, one will never be able to explain one's action by reference to a given and specific human nature; in other words there is no determinism- man is free man is freedom.*[151]

Although previously it has been explained that freedom arises out of nothingness but in this section we will go through Sartre's concept of freedom, as he compares it with the question that arises out of the argument which goes between determinism and free-will.

Freedom and Action

According to Sartre it can be decided when we understand the nature of an act. As man is basically an active being, we can unfold the basic nature of an act. An act is capable of modifying the shape of the world. To act is to arrange means in the view of an end.

The very first idea about an act is that an action on

principle is intentional. A careless smoker who has through negligence caused the explosion of a powder magazine has not acted. Although the intentional act may produce a lot more results than anticipated but one thing is implied that the action necessarily is based on a 'desideratum'; that is, of an objective lack or again of a 'negative'. In Sartre, consciousness which finds itself as a lack decides a counterweight in the end which is a non-being right now:

> *This means that from the moment of the first conception of the act, consciousness has been able to withdraw itself from the full world of which it is consciousness and to leave the level of being in order frankly to approach that of non-being.*[152]

Sartre explains this by citing an example about suffering. Suppose one worker is suffering in a condition. He suffers without considering his suffering and without conferring value on it. To suffer and to be are one and the same for him. This suffering in on the level of his non-positional consciousness, but he does not contemplate it. So this suffering cannot be a motive of his acts. But once he plans a project to change the situation, his present suffering becomes intolerable to him. So once he gives himself room, he withdraws in relation to it, he brings in affect a double nihilation. On the one hand an ideal state of affairs as a pure present nothingness; on the other hand, the actual situation as nothingness in relation to this state of affairs.

It is clear that as soon as one attributes to consciousness this negative power with respect to the world and itself and nihilation forms an integral part of the positing of an end, we find that, 'the indispensable and fundamental condition of all action is the freedom of acting being'.

The determinist puts stress on cause and motive for

any action and proponents of the free-will give no importance to prior cause or deliberations and tries to find intentional structure on the level of act making the act absurd.

Sartre explains that since every action is intentional: each action must, in fact have an end and the end in turn is referred to a cause. This is indeed the unity of three temporal ekstases. But there is difference between the determinist and the theory of Sartre. Where determinist stops their investigation with the designation of cause and motive, Sartre stresses on the importance of act and explains that motive is an integral part of an act. Each of the three structures [cause-act-motive] claims the two others as its meaning: As Sartre says:

> *The essential question lies beyond the complex organization 'cause-intention-act-end'; indeed we ought to ask how a cause (or motive) can be constituted as such.*[153]

The for-itself must confer on it its values as cause or motive. The motive is understood only by the end; that is by the non-existent. It is therefore in itself a negatite. The motive makes itself understood as what it is by means of the ensemble of beings which 'are not' by ideal existences, and by the future. Just as the future turns back upon the present and the past in order to elucidate them, so it is the ensemble of my projects which turns back in order to confer upon the motive its structure as a motive. It is only because I escape the in-itself by nihilating myself toward my possibilities that this in-itself can take on value as cause or motive. Causes and motives have meaning only inside a projected ensemble which is precisely an ensemble of non-existents. And this ensemble is ultimately myself as transcendence; It is me in so far as I have to be myself outside of myself.

So it is the act which decides its ends and motive and

the act is the expression of freedom. Freedom is the foundation of all essences since man reveals intramundane essences by surpassing the world towards his own possibilities.

The for-itself is conscicusness.This consciousness in its existence, exists as a particular experience of the cogito. This cogito determines the freedom as a freedom which is ours as a pure factual necessity. But experience of being a contingent existent on the level of cogito is implicit as not known to us directly. The thing which is explicit in us is that; I am an existent who learns his freedom through his acts. So my freedom is perpetually in question in my being. It is not a quality added on or a property of my nature. It is exactly the stuff of my being.

Nihilating rupture of the for-itself with the world and with himself is the thing which coincides with freedom. 'Having Been' for the human reality in the form of in-itself, in the form of essence, is nihilated and for-itself escapes its being. This way the for-itself in nothingness finds its freedom in the form of acts which determine for the for-itself a motive or the end. And we say In the for-itself, existence precedes essence.

> *Indeed by the sole fact that I am conscious of the causes which inspire my action, these causes are already transcendent objects for my consciousness: they are outside. In vain shall I seek to catch hold of them; I escape them by my very existence. I am condemned to exist forever beyond my essence, beyond the causes and motives of my act. I am condemned to be free. This means that no limits to my freedom can be found except freedom itself or if you prefer, that we are not free to cease being free.*[154]

Human-reality which fails to recognize its own freedom, seeks to find causes in external reason such as God or nature. Man forgets that causes and motives are not things but they have the meaning which he confers on them. This way we can say that Human reality is a being such that in its being its freedom is at stake because human reality perpetually tries to refuse to recognize its freedom. People posit ends as transcendences, which is not an error. But instead of seeing that the transcendences these posited are maintained in their being by my own transcendence, people will assume that I encounter them upon my surging up in the world; they come from God, from nature, from 'my' nature, from society. These ends ready made and pre-human will therefore define the meaning of my act even before I conceive it, just as causes as pure psychic gives will produce it without my even being aware of them.

Human reality is free because it is not enough. It is free because it is perpetually wrenched away from itself and because it has been separated by a nothingness from what it is and from what it will be. It is free, finally, because its present being is itself a nothingness in the form of the 'reflection-reflecting'.

> *Freedom is precisely the nothingness which is made-to-be at the heart of man and which forces human reality, to be is to choose oneself; nothing comes to it either from the outside or from within which it can receive or accept. Without any help whatsoever, it is entirely abandoned to the intolerable necessity of making itself be-down to the slightest detail. Thus freedom is not a being; it is the being of man.*[155]

Thus Sartre says that there is no reality except in action. Man is nothing else but what he purposes, he exists only in so far as he realises himself, he is therefore nothing else but the sum of his actions, nothing else but what his life is. Now the place of the will is to be decided in the life of the for-itself which exercises its freedom. The will presupposes the foundation of an original freedom in order to be able to constitute itself as will. Freedom is existence of our will or of our passions in so far as this existence is the nihilation of facticity.

The will is determined within the compass of motives and ends already posited by the for-itself in a transcendent projection of itself toward its possibles. The will rejects the magical and will apply itself to realizing determined series and instrumental complexes which will enable us to resolve the problem. It will organize a system of means by taking its stand on instrumental determinism.

Sartre therefore uses the term cause for the objective apprehension of a determined situation as this situation is revealed in the light of a certain end as being able to serve as the means for attaining this end. The motive on the contrary is generally considered as a subjective fact. It is the ensemble of the desires, emotions and passions which urge one to accomplish a certain act.

If we say that the state of affairs is revealed to the for-itself i.e. consciousness or the for-itself is the being by which there is a world means the same. The for-itself which is its own individuality has projected itself in this or that way in order to discover the instrumental complexes. Causes appear in and through the project of an action. The internal organization which consciousness has given to itself in the form of non-positional self-consciousness is strictly correlative with the carving out of causes in the world.

There is no ontological distinction between cause and motive. The cause is objective and the motive is in-itself, they are presented as a dyad in the objective structure of the world. My project confers value on the causes and motives. The choice of deliberation is organized within the ensemble motive-causes and ends by free spontaneity.

Decision is taken when the will intervenes; the value of will is to make the announcement.

Freedom and Choice

The fundamental act of freedom is to choose oneself. It is a choice of me in the world and by the same token it is a discovery of the world. My ultimate and total possibility as the original integration of my entire possibility, and the world as the totality which comes to existents by my upsurge into being are strictly two correlative notions. I can perceive the hammer only on the ground of the world; but conversely I can outline this act of 'hammering' only on the ground of the totality of myself and in terms of that totality.

> *Thus the first phenomenon of being in the world is the original relation between the totality of the in-itself or world and my own totality detotalized; I choose myself as a whole in the world which is a whole. Just as I come from the world to a particular 'this', so I come from myself as a detotalized totality to the outline of one of my particular possibilities 'this' on the ground of the world only on the occasion of a particular project of myself.*[156]

Our choice is always a conscious choice. This consciousness can be only non-positional. It is-we-as-consciousness since it is not distinct from our being. And our being is precisely our original choice; the consciousness (of) the choice is identical with the self-consciousness which we have.

I can assume consciousness of myself only as a particular man engaged in this or that enterprise, anticipating this or that success, and by means of the ensemble of these anticipations, outlining his whole figure. On the other hand the world by means of its very articulation refers to us exactly the image of what we are. We choose the world, not in its contexture as in-itself but in its meaning, by choosing ourselves.

> *The value of things, their instrumental role, their proximity and real distance (which have no relation to their spatial proximity and distance) do nothing more than to outline my image- that is, my choice. My clothing (a uniform or a lounge suit, a soft or a starched shirt) whether neglected as cared for, carefully chosen or ordinary, my furniture, the street on which I live, the city in which I reside, the books with which I surround myself, the recreation which I enjoy, everything which is mine (that is, finally, the world of which I am perfectly conscious, at least by way of a meaning implied by the objet which I look at or used: all this informs me of my choice – that is, my being.*[157]

Fundamental Choice or Original Choice:

Here all this or that choices refer to the fundamental choice or original choice. Our original choice is not effected by causes and motives, in fact it itself creates all motives and causes, which guides us to partial actions; it is this choice which arranges the world with its meaning, its instrumental-complexes and its coefficient of adversity.

Freedom, choice, nihilation, temporalization are all one and the same thing. Our original choice unfolds time and becomes one with the unity of three ekstases. To choose ourselves is to nihilate ourselves that is to cause a future to come to make known to us what we are by conferring a meaning on our past.

Every fundamental choice defines the direction of the pursued-pursuit at the same time that it temporalizes itself. The nihilation is pursued continuously and consequently the free and continuous recovery of the choice is obligatory. This recovery is not made from instant to instant while I freely reasume my choice. There is spontaneous invention of motives and causes, which placed within the compass of my fundamental choice thereby enriches it. Neither my facticity nor the world allows us to understand why I raise this glass rather than that inkwell as a figure raising itself on the ground. These choices are apprehended in terms of the original choice.

The choice of total ends although totally free is not necessarily nor even frequently made in joy. We must not confuse our necessity of choosing with the will to power. The choice can be affected in resignation or uneasiness; it can be a flight; it can be realized in bad faith. We can choose ourselves as fleeing, inapprehensible, as indecisive etc. We can even choose not to choose ourselves. In these various instances, ends are posited beyond a factual situation, and the responsibility for these ends falls on us. Even the person having inferiority complex is living in choice. Sartre says that:

> *At all events the 'inferiority complex' can arise only if it is founded on a free apprehension of our being-for-others.*[158]

If we choose as base or humiliated, we constitute ourselves as a mean of attaining these ends. It frees us from existence-for-itself. It is freeing us from our freedom to the advantage of others. Being-for-itself is completely absorbed by being-for-others in inferiority complex.

The choice of inferiority implies the constant realization of a gap between the end pursued by the Will and the end attained. The one who chooses to be inferior intentionally maintains this gap. It is in bad-faith that is; it flees the recognition of the true ends chosen by the spontaneous consciousness.

Human-reality can choose itself as it intends but is not able not to choose itself. It cannot even refuse to be.

Suicide, in fact, is a choice and affirmation-of being. By this being which is given to it, human reality participates in the universal contingency of being and thereby in what we may call absurdity. It is absurd in this sense-that the choice is that by which all foundations and all reasons come into being; that by which the very notion of the absurd receives a meaning. It is absurd as being beyond all reasons. Thus freedom is not pure and simple contingency in so far as it turns back toward its being in order to illuminate its being in the light of its end. It is the perpetual escape from contingency. It is the interiorization, the nihilation, and the subjectivizing of contingency, which thus modified passes wholly into the gratuity of the choice.

The free project is fundamental, for it is my being. Neither ambition nor the passion to be loved nor the inferiority complex can be considered as fundamental projects. On the contrary, they of necessity must be understood in terms of a primary project which is recognized as the project which can no longer be interpreted in terms of any other and which is total. Fundamental project which I am is a project concerning not my relation with this or that particular object in the world, but my total being-in-the-world. However we need not understood by this that the fundamental project is co-extensive with the entire 'life' of the for-itself. Since freedom is a being-without-support and without a spring-board, the project in order to be, must be constantly renewed. I choose myself perpetually and can never be merely by virtue of having-been-chosen; otherwise I should fall into the pure and simple existence of the in-itself.

The existence of the for-itself in fact conditions its essence. But it is necessary to consult each man's history in order to get from it a particular idea with regard to each individual for-itself. Our particular projects, aimed at the realization in the world of a particular end, are united in the global project which we are. But precisely because we are wholly choice and act, these partial projects are not determined by the global project. They must themselves be choices; and a certain margin of contingency, of unpredictability, and of the absurd is allowed to each of them although each project as it is projected is the specification of the global project on the occasion of particular elements in the situation and so is always understood in relation to the totality of my being-in-the-world.

Freedom and Facticity – The Situation

Sartre explains facticity, including all the facts which are given to the man and are beyond his reach to be defined, he calls it contingency. He says that I am not 'free' either to escape the lot of my class, of my nation, of my family, or even to build up my own power or my fortune or to conquer my most insignificant appetites or habits. I am born a worker, a Frenchman, a hereditary syphilitic, or a tubercular. The history of a life, whatever it may be, is the history of a failure. As facticity is a trouble in the way of freedom thus Sartre calls it the coefficient of adversity of things, and it is such that years of patience are necessary to obtain the feeblest result. So he says that again it is necessary 'to obey nature in order to command it.

> *Much more than he appears 'to make himself', man seems 'to be made' by climate and earth, race and class, language, the history of the collectivity of which he is a part, heredity, the individual circumstances of his childhood, acquired habits, the great and small events of his life.*[159]

This facticity which is in-itself is revealed and utilized by the for-itself. On the one hand it helps the for-itself to authenticate its existence and on the other hand create obstacle in way to exercise its freedom to achieve desired end.

If one imagines what a crag can be in itself, it is neutral. But its manifestation as an end can make it adverse or helpful. Brute things can from the start limit our freedom of action. It is our freedom in fact, which at the first place which constitutes the framework, the technique, and the ends in relation to which they will manifest themselves as limits. The crag manifests a profound resistance if I wish to displace it, it will be on the contrary valuable if I want to climb upon it in order to look over the countryside. Now if it is revealed as 'too difficult to climb'; it is such as because originally my freedom grasped it as climbable. There our freedom constitutes the limits which it will encounter subsequently. This resistance is not a danger to the freedom, it just enables it to rise as freedom. There can be a free for-itself only engaged in a resisting world.

Facticity cannot invalidate freedom, as the for-itself is condemned to freedom, means for-itself, is a freedom which chooses but it cannot choose not to be free. Freedom exists through the supression or nihilation of the given on the part of for-itself. There are thousands of ways which the for-itself has of trying to wrench itself away from its original contingency, which means to practice right and to engage oneself in functional authority etc. to escape the contingency and to prove one's existence. But there effort to escape contingency, establish the existence of contingency. Freedom does not mean determination of an end but it is making the choice of an end.

> *It is simply the pure contingency which freedom exerts by denying the given while making itself choice; the given is the plentitude of being which freedom colors with insufficiency and with*

> *negative by illuminating it with the light of an end which does not exist.*[160]

It depends on the for-itself, who finds causes in the world in the light of his own chosen end. This for-itself when exercising his freedom to nihilitate facticity encounter obstacles, they become purely subjective to him, as for the other the whole situation may be different according to his chosen ends. So the situation which is common product of contingency of the in-itself and of freedom, may vary from man to man. Crag is climbable if I choose to be a mountaineer but a person watching just aesthetic beauty of the landscape will not be concerned to the point whether it is scalable or not.

> *What is an obstacle for me may not be for the other. There is no obstacle in an absolute sense but the obstacle reveals its co-efficient of adversity across freely invented and freely acquired techniques. The obstacle reveals this efficient also in terms of the value of the end posited by freedom.*[161]

In this way we find paradox of freedom: there is freedom only in a situation and there is a situation only through freedom. Human reality everywhere encounters resistances and obstacles have meaning only in and through the free choice which human reality is.

> *What we call the facticity of freedom is the given which it has to be and which it illuminates by its project.*[162]

Sartre expresses the given is in the form of the place, the body, the past, the position in so far as it is already determined by the indication of others, and finally the fundamental relation of the for-itself to the other, none of them appear although alone. All of them combined make the situation.

The Place:

Sartre expresses the fact of the place as follows:

> *It is naturally the spot in which I 'live' (my 'country') with its sun, its climate, its resources, its hydrographic and orographic configuration). It is also more simply the arrangement and the order of the objects which at present appear to me (a table, beyond the table a window, to the left of the window a cabinet, to the right a chair, and beyond the window the street and the sea), which indicate me as the reason for their order.*[163]

He says that my birth place which was chosen by my parents, may for insignificant reasons, is received by me as the original place. To be born is, to take one's place, and throughout life I will occupy other places in terms of it. My place will be considered as absolute extension, that is, that which is defined by my place considered as the center for which distances are accounted for absolutely, with me as object and without reciprocity. The only absolute extension is that which unfolds starting from a location which I am absolutely.

To be in place is to be far from-or-near to - that is, place is provided with a meaning in relation to a certain not-yet-existing being which one wants to attain. It is the accessibility or the inaccessibility of this end which defines place. It is therefore in the light of not-being and of the future that my position can be understood.

> *Projected future-intervenes everywhere. It is my future life at Bordeaux, at Etaples, the future discharge of the solider – it is all this which means my place to me and which makes me exist with nervousness or impatience or nostalgia.*[164]

Thus the facticity of the place is revealed to a person only in and through the free choice which he makes of the end.

It is in relation to my dream of seeing New York that it is absurd and painful for me to live at Mont-de-Marsan.

Sartre says that my engagement gives meaning to my contingent place and which is my freedom. To be sure, in being born I take a place, but I am responsible for the place, which I take. We can see clearly here the inextricable connection of freedom and facticity in the situation. Without facticity freedom would not exist as a power of nihilation and of choice and without freedom facticity would not be discovered and would have no meaning.

The Past:

The past is that part of temporality which has slipped out of hand, but Sartre does not consider it dead as he says that the past is present and melts insensibly into the present; it is the suit of clothes which I selected six months ago, the house which I have built, the book which I began last winter, my wife, the promises which I have made to her, my children : all which I am I have to be in the mode of having been. In this way the past is essence, as the essence is what has been. I can no longer think anything about myself since I think about what I am and since I am in the past. But in the other hand I am the being through whom the past comes to my and to the world.

> *What is, therefore takes on its meaning only when it is surpassed towards the future. Therefore what-is is the past. We see how the past as 'that which is to be changed is indispensable to the choice of the future and how consequently no free surpassing can be effected except in terms of a past.*[165]

The past which is cut from the present loses its meaning, but It does not mean that every act of the past is significant, only the facts which are connected to the future, in and through my fundamental project gain importance as a past of mine. So Sarte says that I alone in fact can decide at each moment the bearing of the past. In this sense the past becomes facticity when it becomes obligatory on the part of the for-itself sometimes to decide in terms of past life. Thus he says that:

> *The engagements which I have undertaken weigh upon me. Of course the marriage I made earlier, the house I bought and furnished last year limit my possibilities and dictate my conduct; but precisely because my projects are such I reassume the marriage contract. In other words, precisely because I do not make of it a "Marriage contract which is past, surpassed, dead" and because on the contrary, my projects imply fidelity to the engagements undertaken or the decision to have an 'honorable life' as a husband and a father, etc., these projects necessarily come to illuminate the past marriage vow and to confer on it its always actual value. Thus the urgency of the past comes from the future.*[166]

Thus like place, the past is integrated with the situation when the for-itself by its choice of the future confers on its past facticity a value, an hierarchical order, and an urgency in terms of which this facticity motivates the act and conduct of the for-itself.

The Environment:

Sartre connects feature of environment not only with the geographical conditions but also with unpredictability of events and acts also. It explains unforeseen in concrete terms. Environment is made up of the instrumental things which surround me, including their peculiar coefficients of adversity and utility. As I can change the appearance of environment, the environment can change or be changed by others without having my hand in it.

> *The fact remains that my field of action is perpetually traversed by the appearances and disappearances of objects with which I have nothing to do.*[167]

Suppose I am involved in the project to go somewhere on my bicycle. Ends are chosen by me, I have apprehension of distance from my place to the town, means adopted by me are well chosen. But in between the journey If I get flat tire of bicycle, sun is too hot, the wind is blowing against me, all the phenomenon which are unforeseen: constitute the environment. All these environmental resistances appear only in the light of my free project, i.e. of the choice of the end which I am.

The very project of a freedom in general is a choice which implies the anticipation and acceptance of some kind of resistance somewhere. The freedom's very project in general to do in a resisting world by means of a victory over the world's resistances so there is always a place for unpredictable in every project. Thus we find a new characteristic of free choice. Every project of freedom is an open project and not a closed project. Although entirely individualized, it contains within it the possibility of its further modifications.

Sartre says that there is nothing unforeseen in the sense of metaphysical value or unpredictability of things. There is nothing which astonishes in the world, nothing which surprises us without our determining ourselves to be surprised. The theme of astonishment is not particular but general in a general world, where we are thrown among a totality of existents thoroughly indifferent to me. Despite of my relations with them, they have relations among themselves also. It is on freely projected meaning of adversity in general that this or that complex can manifest its individual coefficient of adversity.

The Fellowmen:

This point of facticity is referred to the presence pf other people in the world. Sartre explains it saying that:

> *To live in a world haunted by my fellowman is not only to be able to encounter the other at every turn of the road; it is also to find myself engaged in a world in which instrumental complexes can have a meaning which my free project has not given to them. It means also that in the midst of this world already provided with meaning I meet with a meaning which is mine and which I have not given to myself, which I discover that I 'posses already'. Thus what the original and contingent fact of existing in a world in which 'there are' also others can mean for our situation.*[168]

So there exist objective meanings which are given to me as not having been brought to light by me. It means that I am engaged in an already meaningful world, this is understood by me when I live in a city: streets, houses, shops, streetcars and buses, directing signs, warning signs, music on the radio etc. A building is not just brute existent, that may be an apartment house, a shop, a group of offices etc. The meaning is contingent, independent of my choice. Directions, instructions, orders, prohibitions, billboards are addressed to me in so far as I am just anybody. I obey them, just fall into the line, submit to the goals of a human reality which is just anybody and I realize them by just any techniques.

> *Therefore facticity is expressed on this level by the fact of my appearance in a world which is revealed to me only by collective and already constituted techniques which aim at making me apprehend the world in a form whose meaning has been defined outside of me. These techniques are going to determine my belonging to collectivities: to the*

human race, to the national collectivity, to the professional and to the family group.[169]

For-itself cannot be a person i.e. choose the ends which it is – without being a man or woman, a member of a national collectivity, of a class, of family etc. Encountered with a prohibition in his path ['No Jews allowed here', or 'Jewish Restaurant), the person is referred to the collective techniques. Now it depends on his free choice and possibilities which decide that he can disobey it, pay no attention to it. But these external limits of freedom will never be either a real obstacle for freedom or a limit suffered. Freedom is total and infinite. The only limit which freedom encounters is that which it imposes on itself in the realization of choices.

The Death:

Death is a being which belongs to an existent process and which in a certain way constitutes the meaning of the process. Death has always been considered as the final boundary of human life.

It is nothing but the revelation of the absurdity of every expectation even though it be the expectation of death itself.[170]

Sartre says that the possibility of my death means only that I am biologically only a relatively closed, relatively isolated system; it indicates only the fact that my body belongs to the totality of existents. Practically I can die at the age of thirty seven or at the age of a hundred. We have every chance of dying before we have accomplished our task.

Thus this perpetual appearance of chance at the heart of my projects cannot be apprehended as my possibility but, on the contrary, as the nihilation of all my possibilities, a nihilation which itself is no longer a part of my possibilities.[171]

According to Sartre the death brings an end to the life at any unpredictable moment, thus revealing absurdity of life. If it is the closing of the account which gives our life its meaning and its value, then it is of little importance that all the acts of which the web of our life is made have been free. The very meaning of them escapes us if we do not ourselves choose the moment at which the account will be closed.

The unique characteristic of a dead life is that it is a life of which the other makes himself the guardian. In reality death is the relation which we would call 'being-for-others'. In its upsurge into being, the for-itself must assume a position in relation to the dead; this initial project organizes the dead in a large anonymous mass or as distinct individuals.

> *It is I, it is the men of my generation who decide the meaning of the efforts and the enterprises of the preceding generation whether we resume and continue their social and political attempts, or whether we realize a decisive rupture and throw the dead back to inefficacy.*[172]

Man lives in the subjectivity and protects it against all exteriorization when he is living, but death reapprehends all this subjective, depriving it of all subjective meanings and hands it over to the objective. Meaning which the other confers on it according to his wish. So we can say that to be dead is to be pray for the living.

Sartre says that death is not my possibility, toward which I would thrust myself, I cannot wait for it. So we can say that it does not belong to the ontological structure of the for-itself. As it is a triumph of the other over me, it refers to a fact. As the other's existence is a contingent fact death also becomes a contingent fact. The fact of contingency puts death out of reach of all ontological conjectures. To consider one's life in terms of death is to contemplate my subjectivity with point of view of others which is not possible.

> *Death is a pure fact as is birth; it comes to us from outside and it transforms us into the outside. At bottom it is in no way distinguished from birth, and it is the identity of birth and death that we call facticity.*[173]

The death in general would means finite life but Sartre defines it otherwise. He says that finitude is an ontological structure of the for-itself which determines freedom and exists only in and through the free project of the end which makes my being known to me. To be finite, in fact, is to choose oneself; that is, to make known to oneself what one is by projecting oneself toward one possible to the exclusion of others.

The very act of freedom is therefore the assumption and creation of finitude. If I were immortal, it would be forbidden me to 'recover my stroke': it is the irreversibility of temporality which forbids me, and this irreversibility is nothing but the peculiar character of a freedom which temporalizes itself.

Death is an external and factual limit to the subjectivity of the for-itself. In this way death never binds the freedom as the freedom which is individual and subjective freedom remains total and infinite. It does not mean saying that death does not limit freedom but the reason is that freedom never encounters this limit.

The Situation:

Descriptions of the place, the past, the environment, the death and the fellowman serve to help us find the meaning of 'situation' and 'being-in-situation' which characterizes the for-itself in so far as it is responsible for its manner of being without being the foundation of its being. Sartre lays down following points to explain it:

1. I am an existent in the midst of other existents. It means I choose myself-not in my being but in the manner of my being. My position in the midst of the world is defined by instrumental utility and adversity of my surrounding existents in the light of my nihilating self, internal negation of in-itself and freely projected end. This is what we mean by the situation.
2. The situation is neither subjective nor objective, it is a relation of being between a for-itself, and the in-itself which the for-itself nihilates. It is the total facticity, the absolute contingency of the world, of birth, of place, of past, of environment, of the fact of fellowmen and it is the freedom without limits as that which causes there to be a facticity.
3. Meaning of situation differs from person to person. We take two persons in the one situation, a master and a slave .They will take on its meaning only for the for-itself in situation and in terms of the free choice of their ends. Comparison is possible only by a third person who deals with them in objective terms in the midst of the world and in the light of a freely chosen project for himself.
4. Situation is always concrete and given and not abstract and universal. It is clear that ends which are chosen by the for-itself are based on concrete and surpassing of this given.
5. Situation stems from the illumination of the constraint by freedom which gives to it its meaning as constraint.
6. It is the situation which must account for that substantial permanence which we radically recognize in people and which the person experiences empirically in most cases as being his own.

Outer environment may change making our situation simplified or complicated but the original project of the for-itself remains the same.

Freedom and Responsibility

For Sartre freedom being absolute for man, the man carries the weight of the whole world on his shoulders. He is responsible for the world and for himself as a way of being.

> *We are taking the word 'responsibility' in its ordinary sense as "consciousness (of) being the incontestable author of an event or of an object." In this sense the responsibility of the for-itself is overwhelming since he is the one by whom it happens that there is a world; since he is also the one who makes himself be, then whatever may be the situation in which he finds himself, the for-itself must wholly assume this situation with its peculiar coefficient of adversity, even though it be in-supportable. He must assume the situation with the proud consciousness of being the author of it, for the very worst disadvantages or the worst threats which can endanger my person have meaning only in and through my project and it is on the ground of the engagement which I am that they appear. It is therefore senseless to think of complaining since nothing foreign has decided what we feel, what we live, or what we are.*[174]

This is consequence of exercising our freedom that we say that what happens to me is mine. I am always equal to what happens to me qua men, for what happens to a man through other men and through himself can be only human. Even the wars, tortures do not depict non-human situation. It is through fear, flight and recourse to magical types of conduct that we decide on the non-human, but this decision is human and man carries the entire responsibility for it. The whole situation (which is image of my free choice of myself and what it presents to me) is mine it represent me and symbolizes me. The peculiar character of human-reality is that it is without excuse.

> *I must be without remorse or regrets as I am without excuse, for from the instant of my upsurge into being, I carry the weight of the world by myself alone without anything or any person being able to lighten it.*[175]

Sartre says that I am not responsible for the fact that I am born in this or that situation, but I am responsible for it, the way I take it for the projective reconstruction of my for-itself, whether I am ashamed of being born or I am astonished at it or I rejoice over it. Thus in a certain sense I choose being born. The facticity is everywhere but inapprehensible, I never encounter anything except my responsibility.

The responsibility of the for-itself is not only for himself but to the entire world as it is a peopled world and the for-itself in his projects utilizes other as transcendence-transcended, in the instrumental-complex. In the Existentialism is a Humanism he writes that:

> *Our responsibility is thus much greater than we had supposed, for it concerns mankind as a whole. I am hereby committing not only myself, but humanity as a whole. I am thus responsible for myself and for all men, and I am creating a certain image of man as I would have him to be.*[176]

Existential Psychoanalysis

In this section Sartre makes explicit the goal of human life, which is outcome of the absolute freedom of man. The ontological description of man ends here, as according to Sartre next step is up to psychological investigation. Human reality identifies and defines itself by the ends which it pursues. There is naturally infinity of possible projects as there is infinity of possible human beings. The fundamental project of being is not different from the being of the for-itself. To the for-itself being means to make known to oneself what one is by means of a possibility appearing as value. Ontologically the for-itself is a lack of being. So value haunts the for-itself as the totality of being which is lacking. Fundamentally man is the desire to be, and desire is a lack. Original project of the man is thus project of being. Sartre explains it as such:

> *The for-itself is the being which is to itself its own lack of being. The being which the for-itself lacks is the in-itself. The for-itself arises as the nihilation of the in-itself and this nihilation is defined as the project toward the in-itself. Between the nihilated in-itself and projected in-itself the for-itself is nothingness. Thus the end and the goal of the nihilation which I am, is the in-itself. Thus human reality is the desire of the being-in-itself. But the in-itself which it desires cannot be pure contingent, absurd in-itself, comparable at every point to that which it encounters and which it nihilates – what the for-itself demand of the in-itself is precisely the totality detotalized – "in-itself nihilated in for-itself". That is why the possible is projected in general as what the for-itself lacks in order to become in-itself-for-itself. The ideal of consciousness which would be the foundation of its own being-in-itself, can be called God. Thus the best way to conceive of the fundamental project of human-reality is to say that man is the being whose project is to be God. If man posses a pre-ontological comprehension of the being of God. God value and supreme end of transcendence represent the permanent limit in terms of which man makes known to himself what*

> *he is. To be man means to reach beyond towards being God. Or if you prefer man fundamentally is the desire to be God.*[177]

We say that meaning of desire is the project of being God, the desired in fact is not constituted by this meaning but it is particular discovery of this end. Sartre here connects his ontology with the concrete projects of a man as man is not just a theory but actual life. The desire of being in its abstract purity is the truth of the concrete fundamental desires. Thus the fundamental project, the person, the free realization of human truth is everywhere in all desires.

Sartre suggests an enquiry through the concrete projects of man to understand the being of man. A specific method for this is named by Sartre as existential psychoanalysis. It includes making a catalogue of empirical desires, which are to be made the object of appropriate psychological investigations, observation and induction and as needed, experience can serve to draw up this list.

The principle of this psychoanalysis is that man is a totality and not a collection. The man expresses as a whole in even his most insignificant and his most superficial behavior, a clue to his Being. In other words every taste, every mannerism and every human act is revealing.Thus the goal of psychoanalysis is to decipher the empirical behavior patterns of man and to fix them conceptually.

Existential psychoanalysis seeks to determine the original choice. It decides the attitude of a person when confronted with logic and principles. It brings together in a pre-logical synthesis of the totality of the existent. It grasps the concrete behaviour that is the specific desire with its entire characteristic network.

The projects revealed by the existential psychoanalysis will be apprehended from the point of view of the other. Thus the object brought into light will be articulated according to the structures of the transcended-transcendence; that is its being will be being-for-others even if the psychoanalyst and the subject of the psychoanalysis are actually the same person.

> *Choice is nothing but the being of human reality; this amounts to saying that a particular partial behavior is or expresses the original choice of this human reality. Since for human reality there is no difference between existing and choosing for itself.*[178]

The goal of inquiry must be to discover a choice and not a state; Investigator should keep in mind that his object is a free, conscious determination. The method which serves for one person may not be suitable another or for the same subject at a later period.

> *It is a method destined to bring to light, in a strictly objective form, the subjective choice by which each living person makes himself a person; that is makes known to himself what he is. Since what the method seeks is a choice of being at the same time as a being. It must reduce particular behaviour patterns to fundamental relations, not of sociality of the will to power, but of being.*[179]

It seeks to detach being from its symbolic expressions, it will have to rediscover each time on the basis of a comparative study of acts and attitudes, a symbol destined to decipher them. It's criterion of success will be number of facts which its hypothesis permits it to explain and to unify as well as the self-evident intuition of the irreducibility of the end attained. The most important symbol to express the being of man would be possessions of man in the ways of doing and having. Sartre explains it in the following manner:

Possession

Possessions are to be found through concrete desires. The information which ontology can furnish concerning behaviour patterns and desires must serve as the basic principles of existential psychoanalysis. It does not mean that there is an overall pattern of abstract desires common to all men: it means that concrete desires have structures which emerge during the study of ontology as these concrete desires express all human reality. Thus according to Sartre, final discoveries of ontology are the first principles of psychoanalysis.

Human reality is expressed by concrete desires, as that of eating, drinking, sleeping, creating something etc. Individual desire considered will not furnish any knowledge and result, but as man is a totality, all desires are to be viewed for laying down base for the existential psychoanalysis..

Actually a thousand empirical examples show that we desire to possess this object or to do that thing or to be someone. If I desire this picture, it means that I desire to buy it, to appropriate it for myself. If I dress-up, it is because I desire to be well-groomed.

> *Thus from the outset, the three categories of concrete human existence appear to us in their original relation: to do, to have to be.*[180]

To know is one of the forms which can be assumed by to have an Idea of discovery of revelation, it also includes an idea of appropriative enjoyment. When a man is praying, bent on discovering himself as free in his very action, he certainly could not be concerned with possessing a being in the world. His goal, which he aims at through sports or pantomime or games, is to attain himself as a certain being, precisely the being which is in question in his being.

> *Art, Science, Play are activities of appropriation, either wholly or in past and what they want to appropriate beyond the concrete object of their quest is being itself, the absolute being of the in-itself. Thus desire is a relation with concrete existent in the midst of the world. And relation of the for-itself to this in-itself is appropriation.*[181]

Quality of being possessed does not indicate a purely external relation to the possessor, this quality affects its very depths. The expression for this internal relation is called appropriation; to be possessed means to be for someone. This means that possessed subject is touched in its being. Thus can be said that desire of a particular object is not the simple desire of this object; it is the desire to be united with the object in an internal relation. There are other appropriation acts also other than possession. Destruction is such an act. The for-itself has violent urge to destroy the possessed object. Sartre says that:

> *Destruction then is to be given a place among appropriative behaviors – to consume is to annihilate and it is to eat: it is to destroy by incorporating into oneself.*[182]

To possess is to wish to possess the world across a particular object. And as possession is defined as the effect to apprehend ourselves as the foundation of a being in so far as it is ourselves ideally, every possessive project aims at constituting the for-itself as the foundation of the world or a concrete totality of the in-itself, and this totality is, as totality, the for-itself existing in the mode of in-itself.

Thus the desire can be either the desire to be or the desire to have. Desire to have is not irreducible. Sartre combines them and says that we have to do with two ways of looking forward to the single goal. The one tending to confer being on the for-itself without detour, the other establishing the circuit of selfness, that is, inserting the world between the for-itself and its being. It is lack of being which I am but the being, of which I make myself a lack is strictly individual and concrete. Thus the very nihilation which I am is individual and concrete. Every for-itself is a choice and each of its acts express this choice, this is called freedom. So finally we can say what is choice; "It is choice of being"; either directly or by appropriation of the world. Sartre says:

> *Freedom is a choice of being 'God', and all my acts, all my projects translate this choice, and reflect it in a thousand and one ways. For there is infinity of ways of being and of having.*[183]

To choose the being is to possess the world through its particular objects. In it we aim at the being of object through its mode of being or quality. It is man who gives the world its meaning. Finally Sartre concludes about his ontology like this:

> *Every human reality is a passion in that it projects losing itself so as to found being and by the same stroke to constitute the in-itself, which escapes contingency by being its own foundation, the Ens causa sui, which religions call God. Thus the passion of man is the reverse of that of Christ; for man loses himself as man in order that God may be born. But the idea of God is contradictory and we lose ourselves in vain. Man is a useless passion.*[184]

Implications of Ontology

Implications of ontology means that how can the ontological study of man will be helpful to decipher codes related to various fields. Such as we would go through metaphysical and ethical implications as explained by Sartre himself.

Metaphysical Implications

Sartre tried to find metphysical implications of his ontology. He said that the for-itself and in-itself are reunited by a synthetic connection which is nothing other than the for-itself, itself. The for-itself is the nihilation of the in-itself. It is like a hole in being at the heart of being. The for-itself is like tiny nihilation which has its origin, at the heart of being; and this nihilation is sufficient to cause a total upheaval to happen to the in-itself and Sartre calls this upheaval the world. According to Sartre consciousness is a revealing intuition of something. The consciousness which is for-itself; its being is never given but interrogated since it is always separated from itself by a nothingness of otherness. The for-itself is always suspense because its being is a perpetual reprieve, means the fot-itself is always in the becoming process. If It could ever join with its being, then the otherness would disappear and along with it the possiblities, knowledge and the world. And he resolves the problem of knowledge by establishing the ontological primacy of in-itself over for-itself. Now metaphysical interrogation makes it place here.

> *Metaphysics is the study of individual processes which have given birth to this world as a concrete and particular totality. In this sense metaphysics is to ontology as history is to sociology.*[185]

Two metaphysical questions arise; why does the for-itself arise in terms of being? Why is it that there is being? The first question is devoid of meaning. All the 'whys' in fact are subsequent to being and presuppose it. Being is without reason, without cause and without necessity; the very definition of being releases to us its original contingency.

The second question is not posited on the metaphysical level but on the ontological level. Sartre says that there is being, because the for-itself is such that there is Being and the characteristics of phenomenon comes to Being through the for-itself. Sartre solves the whole problem by establishing weight on ontology rather than on metaphysics. He says that:

> *Questions on the origin of being or on the origin of the world are either devoid of Meaning or receive a reply within the actual province of ontology; the case is not same for the origin of for-itself. The for-itself is such that it has right to turn back on itself towards its own origin. The being by which the 'why' comes into being has the right to posit its own 'why' since it is itself an interrogation, a 'why'.*[186]

Ethical implications

The ontological outcome of man is in terms of absolute freedom and this freedom is defined by Sartre as action on the part of man, and action finds its validity only in the field of morality. Thus we can say that ontology has its implication in the ethical realm. Good or bad which is assigned to the realm of ethics, although do not come directly in the realm of ontology but ontological structure of the for-itself can serve as a clue to understand value. Sartre explains it as such:

> *Ontology has revealed to us in fact that, the origin and the nature of value; we have seen that value is the lack in relation to which the for-itself determines its being as a lack. Various tasks of the for-itself can be made the object of an existential psychoanalysis, for they all aim at producing the missing synthesis of consciousness and being in the form of value or self-cause. Thus existential psychoanalysis is moral description, for it releases to us the ethical meaning of various human projects.*[187]

Sartre further explains that by making men realize their real goal of pursuit, existential psychoanalysis describes their real connection with in-itself. People refrain from appropriating things for their own sake and try to realize the symbolic appropriation of their being-in-itself. Both ontology and existential psychoanalysis make men realize that, "he is the being by whom values exist."

Sartre puts a lot of questions, in the fashion of Socrates, to make it clear that the for-itself and its freedom are not like in-itself.

> *Freedom is always at a distance from itself and are described in the form of "being-which-is-not-what-it-is" and 'which-is-what-it-is-not', and this freedom chooses as the ideal of being, "being-what-it-is-not and not-being-what-it-is." This emptiness or nothingness replies to us in terms of Ethics.*[188]

In his lecture named Existentialism is a Humanism Sartre makes the point of ethics very clear. He says that his existentialism is not a self centered philosophy but is humanism. This humanistic approach of existentialism, explains it as the most optimistic discipline. According to Sartre it is optimism that confronts man with a possibility of choice. It means a free, responsible man who decides humanity in his subjectivity and it happens because the Man is responsible for what he is. Existentialism is a doctrine which affirms that every truth and every action implies both an environment and a human subjectivity.

Ontological description of being affirms that existence is prior to essence. This precedence of existence over essence is atheistic principle and it proves that every act and doctrine should originate from an active being, the man. Sartre says that:

> *When we think of God as the creator, we are thinking of him as a supernal artisan. So when God creates he knows precisely what he is creating. Thus the conception of man in the mind of God is comparable to that of the paper-knife in the mind of the artisan: God makes man according to a procedure and a conception, exactly as the artisan manufactures the paper-knife, following a definition and formula. Thus each individual man is the realization of a certain conception which dwells in the divine understanding. In the philosophical atheism of eighteenth century, the notion of God is surpassed, atheistic existentialism, of which I am a representative, declares that if God does not exist there is at least one being whose existence comes before its essence, a being which exist before it can be defined by any conception of it. That being is man or, as Heidegger has it, the human reality.*[189]

Although ontological description of man as for-itself seems to be shut up within himself but his absolute freedom and his relation with others, describes him as an ethical being. The ethical implications of phenomenological ontology are what Sartre describes as humanism. He says that:

> *Man first of all exists, encounters himself, surges up in the world – and defines himself afterwards. There is no human nature, because there is no God to have a conception of it. Man simply is. Not that he is simply what he conceives himself to be he is what he wills. Man is nothing else but that which he makes of himself. That is the first principle of existentialism.*[190]

Thus nonexistence of the creator demands for someone to invent values. Thus we have to take things as they are.

Life is nothing until it is lived and the value of it is nothing else but resides in the choice; Choice brings along with it, sense of responsibility. Although decisions are purely subjective but area of responsibility is not limited to subjective level as it expands toward whole mankind. Sartre says that man is not only responsible for his individuality, but for all men.

To choose between this or that is at the same time to affirm the value of that which is chosen; for man is unable to choose the worse. What we choose is always the better for all and nothing can be better for us unless it is better for all. So responsibility carries much greater meaning, for it concerns mankind as a whole. I am hereby committing not only myself, but humanity as a whole. In this sense I am creating a certain image of Man as I would have him to be. According to Sartre In fashioning myself I fashion man.

Ethical implications explain ethical and social man moving from subjective values to objective values. As humanism explains ethical, Sartre's humanism is based on subjective efforts and goes to the objective. He criticizes humanity, which is based on absolute values and where man follows realm of objectivity.

> *Thus we have neither behind us, nor before us in a luminous realm of values, any means of justification or excuse. We are left alone, without excuse. That is what I mean when I say that man is condemned to be free. Condemned, because he did not create himself, yet is nevertheless at liberty, and from the moment that he is thrown into this world he is responsible for everything he does.*[191]

The meaning is simple, we are free, therefore we choose – that is to say, we invent. There are no rules of general morality to show us what we ought to do: no signs are vouchsafed in this world. Our aim is precisely to establish the human kingdom as a pattern of values in distinction from the material world. But the subjectivity which we thus postulate as the standard of truth is no narrowly individual subjectivism, for as we have demonstrated, it is not only one's own self that one discovers in the cogito, but those of others too.

Ontological explanation explains that we are just as certain of the other as we are of ourselves. Thus the man who discovers himself directly in the cogito also discovers all the others, and discovers them as the condition of his own existence. The revelation of the other as a freedom, which confronts mine freedom, and which cannot think or will without doing so either for or against me. Thus, at once, man finds him in a world which is that of inter-subjectivity. This inter-subjectivity tells that every purpose, however individual it may be, is of universal value.

Existentialism, carries the absolute character of the free commitment, by which every man realises himself in realising a type of humanity and it bears upon the relativity of the cultural pattern which may result from such absolute commitment.

This commitment gets reality in action only. Sartre says that reality means sum of appearances, in this way man is a totality, described through sum of his actions. Ontological description of the for-itself explains that man is a perpetual striving toward the end or purpose. Man is never complete. In this stream he criticized humanism in the novel Nausea as a form; where a general judgment upon man can be made. Man is all the time outside of himself: it is in projecting and losing himself beyond himself that he makes man to exist; and, on the other hand, it is by pursuing transcendent aims that he himself is able to exist. Since man is thus self-surpassing, and can grasp objects only in relation to his self-surpassing, he is himself the heart and centre of his transcendence.

> *There is no other universe except the human universe, the universe of human subjectivity. This relation of transcendence as constitutive of man with subjectivity (in such a sense that man is not shut up in himself but forever present in a human universe) – it is this that we call 'Existential Humanism'. This is humanism, because we remind man that there is no legislator but himself; that he himself, thus abandoned, must decide for himself; also because we show that it is not by turning back upon himself, but always by seeking, beyond himself, an aim which is one of liberation or of some particular realization, that man can realize himself as truly human.*[192]

Existentialism of Sartre is not atheist in the sense that it would exhaust itself in demonstrations of the non-existence of God. He says, it declares, rather, that even if God existed that would make no difference from its point of view. Not that we believe that God does exist, but we think that the real problem is not that of His existence; what man needs is to find himself again and to understand that nothing can save him from himself, not even a valid proof of the existence of God. In this sense existentialism is optimistic; it is a doctrine of action.

Chapter-4
Man as a Social Being

From Ontology to Sociology

A change in the philosophy of Sartre had taken place with an essay The Search for a Method (1957) and later in The Critique of Dialectical Reason (1960). Now his philosophy was not only ontological but Sociological to a great extent and he defined his man in relation to social structure and economic terms under the influence of Marxism or we can say that his theoretical man was now a practical man, facing the world with real problems. Sartre claimed that:

> *He is 'no one in particular', he is recognizing that the distorting movement of reflection with, which he, as a bourgeois intellectual, has 'turned back' on himself, has merely twisted certain threads in the social fabric; he can also therefore recognize that he is 'everyman.*[193]

Sartre's description of the social man is dialectical. In the Critique he calls it totalizing activity, in which the preceding moments are particular and incomplete relationships within the whole, which are grasped by dialectical reason. In his ontology the 'consciousness of something' and 'self-consciousness' referred to the for-itself. In later philosophy he took it to explain human behaviour; where consciousness of oneself as something is only a particular and dialectically incomplete moment in one's relationship to the other and that consciousness itself is only a particular and dialectically incomplete moment in the course of the action in which it is embodied.

His Search for a Method which served as a preface to The Critique of Dialectical Reason shows how his philosophy reached to 'praxis' from existentialist 'acting and making'. Sartre gives one example when someone crosses a room to open a window. It depicts its intentional consciousness, which after finding the room 'too warm' is set into action. This action defines the agent's situation and the agent himself. Here the term, 'consciousness is consciousness of something' is explained in the same manner as it is explained in Being and Nothingness but window itself is the product of an intentional action: structure of the window indicates that the worker who has made it was conscious of it as something to be pushed up or down or to be swung out. He did not make it his own, thus not expressing his intentions. It is explained by Sartre as such:

> *It is simply the dialectical movement which explains the act by arriving at its terminal signification from its starting conditions. The movement is originally progressive. If my companion suddenly goes toward the window, I understand this gesture in terms of the material situation in which we both are. There is present here a synthetic mode of behavior which, is unifying itself, unifies before my eyes the practical field in which we both are. The movements are new; they are adapted to the situation, to particular obstacles. This is because the psychological sets are abstract adjustments which are insufficiently determinate; they become determined within the unity of the undertaking. I must myself experience the transcending of our material situation. Within the room, doors and*

> *windows are never entirely passive realities; the work of others has given them their meaning, has made out of them instruments, possibilities for an other (any other). This means that I understand them already as instrumental structures and as products of a directed activity. My companion's behavior reveals to me as a 'hodological space' and conversely the indications latent in the instruments become the crystallized meaning which allow me to understand his undertaking. His behaviour unifies the room, and the room defines his behaviour.*[194]

Experience of things is far harder in the Critique than it is in Nausea. Things are heavy with meaning, 'consciousness of something' as consciousness of the use to which it is to be put, is now its deeply 'incised' structure. Things are so much emphasized that our very existence depend on them. Feeling of existence continues to be de trop in the Critique as it was in Nausea.

> *This superfluousness is no longer the meaningless, nauseous proliferation of shapeless existences, overflowing my consciousness of them. I am now conscious of my existence as rendered superfluous by the scarcity of the things on which it depends. Instead of the metaphor of indignation in Nausea, we are faced with actual hunger.*[195]

In critique the fact that what is lacking and valuable is something scarce, imposes a materialistic dialectic in which the technological mode of production is basic and some anonymous material product intervenes as the alienating factor that determines my relation to me as well as to others. Sartre quotes one example:

> *Waiting for the bus, I am conscious, not only for it, but also of its making me something other than*

> *myself: I become an anonymous individual who has taken his place in quantitative 'series' whose inert members are only passively and externally related to each other, by means of the bus for which we are waiting. My interest in the bus is identical with the other's interest, and therefore antithetical, since the scarcity of the places in the bus may render me de trop, and the decision as to who finds a place is reached by a numerical sequence, that requires no reference to the personal values, for which I wrestled with the other in Being and Nothingness.*[196]

Sartre's analysis is phenomenological and for Sartre scarcity is fundamental fact of all human existence. This phenomenological analysis holds for all social history. Analysis of consciousness in Being and Nothingness and analysis of social structures in The Critique of Dialectical Reason is same and based on distinction between two moments i.e. the intentional and the reflexive moments.

Because we are men and because we live in the world of men, of work, and of conflict, all the objects which surround us are signs. By themselves they indicate their use and scarcely mask the real project of those who have made them such for us and who address us through them. But their particular arrangement, retraces for us an individual action, a project, an event.

Everything at every instant is always signifying and significations reveal to us men and relations among men mediated by our structures of our society. But these significations appear to us only insofar as we ourselves are signifying. Our understanding of the other is never contemplative; it is only a moment of our praxis, a way of living; in conflict or in complicity, and the concrete human relations which unite us to him. Some significations refer us to a lived situation, to a specific action, to a social event. Some are symbols; the reality signified is present in them as the nation is in the flag.

According to Sartre observation of social field has revealed that relation of ends is a permanent structure of human undertakings and that it is on the basis of this relation that real men evaluate actions, social and economic institutions. Our understanding of the other is necessarily attained through ends. For example, In order to fight, to outwit the opponent, a person must have at his disposal systems of ends at once.

Explaining his theory Sartre explains about capital market as an end to which all social activities are directed. He says that in a society which is wholly alienated, in which capital appear more and more as a social power of which the capitalist is the functionary.

> *The end as the signification of the lived project of a man or of a group of men remain real to the extent that, as Hegel said, the appearance possesses a reality as appearance. It's rŏle and its practical efficacy, in this last case as well as in the preceding, needs to be specified.*[197]

Dialectical reason

Sartre says that the whole social network of man is to be understood through dialectical reason. The dialectical reason of man is explained by Sartre through totalizing movement. In it two terms coined by Sartre are "praxis" i.e. practical activity and "practico-Inert" which is inertia of the objects and other kinds of obstacles in the way of praxis. Defining totality Sartre reaches to the praxis and practico-inert like this.

> *Totality is defined by Sartre as a being, "radically distinct from the sum of its parts, which is complete-in one form or another-in each of these parts, and which relates to itself either through its*

> *relation to one or several of its parts, or else by its relation to the connections that all, or several, of these parts maintains among themselves. It claims the ontological status of the in-itself, or the inert. The synthetic unity which will produce its appearance of totality cannot be an act, but only what remains of a past action.*[198]

Our practical objects-machines, instruments, consumer goods etc. appear as totality because our present action is what gives them the appearance of totalities by reviving, in one way or another, the praxis which attempted to totalize their inertia.

These inert totalities create among men the type of relation which is called the practico-inert. Human objects should be studied in the human world where they receive their practico-inert status. They weigh upon destiny through that contradiction within them which opposes praxis (the labor that has made them and the labor that make use of them) and create inertia.

Synthetic unity of a habitat is not simply the labour that has produced it but also the act of inhabiting it; left to itself it returns to the multiplicity of inertia. Thus the totalization has the same status as the totality. Through the multiplicities, it continues that synthetic labour which makes of each part a manifestation of the whole, and which relates the whole to itself through the mediation of the parts.

The dialectic is a totalizing activity. It has no laws other than the rules that are produced by the totalization in process; these are obviously concerned with the relations between the unification and the unified-that is, the modes of effective presence of a process of becoming which totalizes those parts which are totalized. This totalization is singular adventure under singular conditions. Totalizing adventure produces itself as critical experience of itself at a certain moment of its development. In this singular moment the act endows itself with reflexive character. Thus universals of the dialectic – its principles and its laws of intelligibility are "singularized universals." Thus totalization claims a moment of the critical consciousness, as the necessary avatar of the totalizing praxis, this moment cannot appear at any time, or at any place, whatever. It is conditioned, in its deep reality as well as in the modes of its appearance. Here critical experience does not denote any historical moment, but Sartre makes it clear through the term 'Anyone at all'.

> *Anyone at all means that any one human life whatever, if the historical totalization must be able to occur, is the direct and indirect expression of the whole (the totalizing movement) and of every life, to the exact extent to which this one life opposes itself to everything and everyone.*[199]

Origin of the critical experience is itself dialectical, but also that the appearance in each person of the reflective and critical consciousness defines itself as an individual attempt to grasp, through one's own real life (conceived as an expression of the whole), the moment of historical totalization. Thus in its most immediate and superficial character, the critical experience of totalization is the very life of the investigator, insofar as this life criticizes itself reflectively. In abstract terms this means that only a man living inside a sector of totalization may grasp the internal relations which unite him with the totalizing movement.

It is a question of the critical experience being brought to bear upon the nature of the links of interiority starting from the human relations which define the investigator. If he is to be totalized by history, what is important here is to relieve his affiliations with human groups of different structures, and to determine the reality of these groups, through the links that constitute them and the practices that define them. And to the very extent that he, personally, is the living mediation between these heterogeneous groups (as, also is any individual whatever), his critical experience must discover if this mediating bond is itself an expression of totalization.

In a word the investigator must, if the unity of history exists, grasps his own life as a whole and the part, as the link between the parts and the whole, and as the relation of the parts among themselves, in the dialectical movement of unification. He must be able to make the leap from his own singular life to history, by the simple practical negation of that negation which determines it. That is tantamount to saying that the individual the questioner who is questioned – is myself and is no one. Through the lived relationships of affiliations we shall grasp in this self which is disappearing – the dynamic relations of the different social structures, insofar as they are transforming themselves through history. So Sartre states that:

> *The major discovery of the dialectical experience is that 'man is mediated' by things to the exact extent that things are 'mediated by men'. It is what is called dialectical circularity.*[200]

Need

On the most superficial and familiar level, the investigation first reveals, in the unity of dialectical connections, unification as the movement of dialectical connections, unification as the movement of individual praxis, plurality, the organization of plurality, and the plurality of organization: The entire historical dialectical rests on the individual praxis in so far as it is already dialectical, that is to say, to the extent that action is itself the negating transcendence of contradiction, the determination of a present totalization in the name of a future totality, and the real effective working of matter. Everything is discoverable in 'Need [*Le besoin*]', this is the first totalizing relation between that material being, a man and the material group to which he belongs. This relation is unilateral, a relation of interiority. Man as a living totality, satisfies its needs in the surrounding materiality. Here material world is infinity as the total field of the possibilities of satisfaction. As man is investigating his critical experience of dialectical reason, it is most convenient to do this in terms of need. As it is need which combines the whole world, which combines the living and non-living.

> *Need (Le besoin) is the first totalising relation between the material being, man and the material ensemble of which he is part. This relation is univocal and of interiority... Need is negation of the negation in so far as it expresses itself as a lack within the organism; and need is a positivity in so far as the organic totality tends to preserve itself as such through it. The original negation is an initial contradiction between the organic and the inorganic, in the last analysis, what is lacking can be reduced to inorganic or less organized elements or quite simply, to dead flesh etc. Thus negation of negation is achieved through the transcendence of the organic towards the inorganic.*[201]

This initial totalisation is transcendent to the extent that the being of the organism lies outside of it, immediately or mediately, in inanimate being;

> *Need sets up the initial contradiction because the organism, in its being, depends directly (oxygen) or indirectly (food), on unorganised being. Everything points to the fact that living bodies*

> *and inanimate objects are made of the same molecules.... It is in terms of total field that need seeks possibilities of satisfaction in nature, and it is thus totalization which will reveal in the passive totality in its own material being as abundance or scarcity.*[202]

Need as a negation of the negation, is the organism itself, living itself in the future, through present disorders as its own impossibility and praxis, in the first instance, is nothing but the relation of the organism, as exterior and future end, to the present organism as a totality under threat; it is function exteriorized. The project, as transcendence, is merely the exteriorization of immanence, transcendence itself is already present in the functional fact of nutrition and excretion, since what we find here is a relation of univocal interiority between two states of materiality. And conversely, transcendence contains immanence within itself in that its link with its purpose and with the environment remains one of exteriorised interiority.

Sartre says that nature, through need combines man and matter in an internal relation. Matter, outside of the body, reduces the body to inorganic status to the same degree that the body transforms matter into a totality. Through just this the body is in danger in the universe; it too harbors the possibility of the organism's non-being. The body in order to stop itself from destruction modifies material world thus It is like a mechanical system.

Labour

Man who produces his life in the unity of the material field, is led by praxis itself to define zones, systems and privileged objects within this inert totality. Thus he sets himself in opposition to himself through the mediation of the inert; and conversely the constructive power of the labourers opposes the part to the whole in the inert within the 'natural' unity. Hence the subsequent task of the labour must be to put the created object back in contact with the other sectors within the whole and to unite them from a new point of view; it negates separation.

Human labour, the original praxis by which man produces and reproduces his life, is entirely dialectical: its possibility and its permanent necessity rest upon the relation of interiority which unites the organism with the environment and upon the deep contradiction between the inorganic and organic orders, both of which are present in everyone. Thus Sartre says:

> *Thus labour organizes itself by synthetic determinations of the ensemble, by discovering or constructing tighter and tighter relations within the practical field so as to convert what was originally only a vague relation of the parts to the whole and to one another into a complete circle of conditioning. To consider an individual at work is a complete abstraction, since in reality labour is as much a relation between men as a relation between man and the material world. Labour considered at the most abstract level, that is as the action of an isolated individual immediately reveals the dialectical character of action.*[203]

Sartre explains as a man from distance, perception of the Other through his labour and the meanings and internal relations it carries along with it.

> *From my window, I can see a road-mender on the road and a gardener working in a garden. Between them there is a wall with bits of broken glass on the top protecting the bourgeois property where the gardener is working. Thus they have no knowledge at all of each other's presence; absorbed*

> *as they are in their work, neither of them even bothers to wonder whether there is anybody on the other side. Meanwhile I can see them without being seen, and my position and this passive view of them at work situates me in relation to them. My initial relation to the two workers is negative; I do not belong to their class, I do not know their trades, I would not know how to do what they are doing, and I do not share their worries.*[204]

In the same example Sartre tries to approach the explanation of the concept of man. Although concept of man does not become clear from these perceptions and he explains that I do not perceive here two men perceived by a man. Because they what they have made themselves through labour and these works define their social relations.

> *The concept of man is an abstraction which never occurs in concrete situation. It is in fact as a holiday maker, confronting a gardener and a road mender, that is I come to conceive myself; and in making myself what I am, I discover them as they make themselves, that is, as their work produces them but to the extent that I cannot see them as ants (as the aesthete does) or as robots (as the neurotic does), and to the extent that I have to project myself through them before their ends, in order to differentiate their ends from mine, I realize myself as a member of a particular society which determines everyone's opportunities and aims; and beyond their present activity, I rediscover their life itself, the relation between needs and wages, and further still, social divisions and class struggles. In this way, the affective quality of my perception depends both on my social and political attitude and on contemporary events.*[205]

The reality of the other affects me in the depths of my being to the extent that it is not my reality. My perception provides me first with a multiplicity of tools and the apparatuses, produced by the labour of others (the wall, the road, the garden, the fields etc.) and it unites them according both to their objective meaning and to my own project. Everything maintains with all its interior the particular unity which a long forgotten action imposed upon it; things in general are indifferent to the living, but ideal act of unification, which I perform in perception.

Reciprocity

From the previous example we see that as perception reveals the dialectical nature of the world, it reveals the relations of reciprocity and the ternary relations also. Neither of them is totalizing. They are multiple adhesions between men which keeps a society in a colloid state.

> *Since it is the same world, they are united, by my personal perception, within the universe as a whole, and in so far as each deprives the other of it. The mere fact, for each of them, of seeing what the other does not see, of exposing the object through a special kind of work, establishes a relation of reciprocity in my perceptual field which transcends my perception: each of them constitutes the ignorance of the other. Of course this mutual ignorance would not come into objective existence without me: the very notion of ignorance presupposes a questioning or knowing third party; otherwise it could be neither experienced nor described; the only real relation would be contiguity, or co-existence in exteriority. But my perception makes me a real and objective mediation between these two molecules.*[206]

The ontological structure working in the concept of 'The

Other' defined by Sartre in the 'Being and Nothingness' plays its part in concrete relations. Sartre says that my subjectivity is objectivity designated by them as other (another class, another profession, etc.) and in interiorising this designation; I become the objective milieu in which these two people realise their mutual dependence outside me. By limiting me each constitutes the limit of the other and deprives him, as he deprives me, of an objective aspect of the world. But this mutual theft is nothing but like the hemorrhage they make in my own perception.

In short, the organization of the practical field in the world determines a real relation for everyone, but one which can only be defined by the experience of all the individuals who figure in this field. This comes down to unification through praxis, and everyone, unifying to the extent that his acts determine a dialectical field, is unified within this field by the unification of the other, that is to say, in accordance with the plurality of unification. The reciprocity of relations is a moment of the contradiction between the unifying unity of praxis and the exteriorising plurality of human organisms.

> *The mutual recognition of two strangers who have just met may seem, it is only the actualisation of a relation which is given as having always existed as the concrete and historical reality of the couple which has just been formed.... In this sense, reciprocity is a permanent structure of every object: defined as things in advance, by collective praxis, we transcend our being by producing ourselves as men among men and we allow ourselves to be integrated by everyone else to the extent that they are to be integrated into our own project. And since the historical content of my project is conditioned by the fact of my already being amongst men and being recognised by them*

> *in advance as a man of a certain kind and milieu, with my place in society already fixed by meanings engraved in matter, reciprocity is always concrete.*[207]

According to Sartre it is the individual which determines his bonds of reciprocity with everyone. But actually this reciprocity comes out as a naked reality of capitalist society where there is actual understanding of freedom and which utilizes need of labour and the whole project becomes a sort of fun of humanity.

> *A swindle of capitalist exploitation is based on a contract. And though this contract necessarily transforms labour, or praxis, into an inert commodity, it is, formally, a reciprocal relation it is a free exchange between two men who recognize each other in their freedom; it is just that one of them pretends not to notice that the other is forced by the constraint of needs to sell himself as a material object. In theory, the employer does not put any pressure on the workers when he hires them, and merely fixes a top rate and turns away those who ask for more. Here, once again, competition and antagonism between workers moderate their demands; the employer himself has nothing to do with it. This example shows clearly enough that man becomes a thing for the other and for himself only to the extent that he is initially posited as human freedom by praxis itself. Absolute respect for the freedom of property less is the best way of leaving him at the mercy of material constraints, at the moment of the contract.*[208]

Reciprocal ternary relations are the basis of all relations between men, whatever form they subsequently take. Though reciprocity is often concealed by the relations which are established and supported by it, it becomes evident whenever it manifests itself that each of the two terms is modified in its very existence by the existence of the other. In other words men are bound together by relations of interiority.

Scarcity

Ontological structure says that desire presupposes lack; likewise dialectical reason presupposes something which produces action in the form of labour, the capitalist and a lot of other acts which somehow humans perform in their lives. Here comes the word scarcity. Sartre description of need gives way to the description of scarcity. This factor of scarcity is revealed when man judges the material environment in terms of need. Sartre explains scarcity as the lived relation of a practical multiplicity with the materiality environing it and within it is the foundation of the possibility of human history.

> *Man is a stunted being mishappen but hardened to suffering who lives to labour from dawn to dusk with these (rudimentary) technical means, on a thankless threatening earth.*[209]

According to Sartre if there is equilibrium between need and a given mode of production, scarcity can be lived (through internal adaptations of the organisms) within certain limits as equilibrium.

> *Scarcity as possibility can be lived within certain limits, as an equilibrium. As long as we remain within this realm, there is no logical (i.e., dialectical) absurdity in conceiving a history-less earth, where human groups would vegetate and never break out of a cycle of repetition, producing their lives with primitive techniques and*

> *instruments and knowing absolutely nothing of one another.*[210]

According to Sartre scarcity is a fundamental relation of our History and a contingent determination of our univocal relation to materiality. But to say that our history is a history of men is equivalent to saying that it is born and developed within the permanent framework of a field of tension produced by scarcity.

> *It is always scarcity, as a real and constant tension both between man and his environment and between man and man which explains fundamental structures (techniques and institutions) not in the sense that it is real force and that it has produced them, but because they were produced in the milieu of scarcity by men and whose praxis interiorize this scarcity even when they try to transcend it. Scarcity is a relation of the individual to the environment. We live in particular situations, the environment is a ready constituted practical field, which relates everyone to collective structures and the most fundamental of these structures is scarcity as the negative unity of the multiplicity of men. This unity is negative in relation to men because it is transmitted to man by matter in so far as matter is non-human.*[211]

This first totalization by materiality appears as the possibility of their destruction. And this destruction happens to man through the praxis of other men.

> *Any natural substance or manufactured product exists, in a specific social field, in insufficient number, given the number of members of the group, or that of the region's inhabitants: there is not enough for everyone. Thus for each person*

> *everyone (the group) exists insofar as the consumption of a certain product there, by others, deprives him here of an opportunity to find and consume an object of the same order.*[212]

Each person within the social field exists and acts in the presence of each and everyone. Although he does not know the number of individuals of society. Common man is not aware of technical of scarcity but he experiences it living in a group. The other men of the group exist together for him. Each of them is a threat to his life or, existence of each man is the interiorization and assumption, by a human life, of the environment as the negation of men. But if the individual member, recognizes himself, through his need and his praxis, as being among men, he discloses each of them in the perspective of the object of consumption or the manufactured product; and on the elementary level on which we are. He discloses each of them as the simple possibility of consuming an object that he needs.

Sartre says that the fact of scarcity shows that all social antagonisms are actually qualified and structured in a given society, the society which itself defines the limits of scarcity for each of the groups that constitute it, and defines itself in the fundamental context of collective scarcity.

> *Scarcity does not express the radical impossibility of the human organism's existence, but in a given situation, scarcity realizes the passive totality of the individuals of a collectivity as the impossibility of coexistence. The group in the nation is defined by its expendables. It must reduce itself numerically to stay alive. For example – one can practice birth control; it is the unborn child, as the future consumer, which is designated as undesirables. It reveals each member of the group simultaneously as a possible survivor*

> *and as an expendable to be disposed of. And thus every person's objectivity is constituted by himself and by everyone.*[213]

Thus it can be said that the individual is challenged by each person in his being, and by the same movement which transcends every challenge. For each person, man exists as inhuman man, as an alien species.

Scarcity says that there is not enough for everybody. In the milieu of scarcity, however, even if individuals are unaware of each other, even of social stratifications and class structures completely sever reciprocity, everyone within the particular social field still exists and acts in the presence of everyone else. The other member of the group do exist for him collectively, in that each one of them is a threat to his life. If this individual member, if he realizes himself, through his need and praxis, as being amongst men, will see everyone in terms of the object of consumption or the manufactured product, and, on this basic level, he will recognize them as the mere possibility of the consumption of something he himself needs. In short he will find each of them to be the material possibility of his being annihilated through the material annihilation of an object of primary necessity.Scarcity makes the passive totality of individuals within a collectivity into an impossibility of co-existence. The group or nation is defined by its surplus population; it has to reduce its number in order to survive.

> *Through socialized matter and through material negation as an inert unity, man is constituted as other than man. Man exists for everyone as non-human man, as an alien species.*[214]

Human relations (positive or negative) are relations of reciprocity; this means that one individuals praxis in its practical structure recognizes, in order to accomplish its purpose, the praxis of the other. Without this human relation of reciprocity, the inhuman relation of scarcity would not exist.

> *In pure reciprocity, what is other than me is also the same. In reciprocity modified by scarcity, the same appears to us as the counter-man, insofar as this same man appears as radically other (that is, as the bearer for us of the threat of death).*[215]

Although all of us have same dialectical structures we find other humans as our demoniac counterpart. Man lives in the terror of his own species in the environment of scarcity.

> *The first movement of the ethical here is the constitution of radical evil and of Manichaeism it appraised and evaluates the rupture of the reciprocity of immanence by interiorized scarcity; but it does so by grasping it as a product of the praxis of the other.*[216]

It gives way to destruction. The ethical at this place reveals itself as a destructive imperative, as evil must be destroyed. One must define violence as a structure of human action under the sway of Manichaeism and in the context of scarcity. Violence claims always to be counter-violence, that is, retaliation to the violence of the other.

> *Whether it is a question of killing, torturing, enslaving or merely mystifying, my goal is to do away with alien liberty as a hostile force, that is, as that force which can repulse me from the practical field and make of me an individual who is 'superfluous' [de trop], condemned to death. In other words it is man qua man, that is, as free praxis of an organized being, that I am attacking; It is man and nothing else that I hate in the enemy – that is, myself as other (and it is certainly I whom I wish to destroy in him) in order to*

> *prevent him from destroying me, actually, in my body.*[217]

Human relations are reciprocal. This means that each individual's praxis, in its practical structure and for the sake of the completion of its project, recognizes the praxis of the other, which means, basically, that it sees the duality of activities as inessential and the unity of praxis as such as essential to them. I do not claim that the relation of reciprocity ever existed in man before the relation of scarcity, man being, after all, the historical product of scarcity. But without this human relation of reciprocity the non-human relation of scarcity would not exist. And everyone interiorizes this structure in that by his behaviour he makes himself a man of scarcity.

Nothing not even wild beasts or microbes could be more terrifying for man than a species which is intelligent, carnivorous and cruel and which can understand and outwit human intelligence, and whose aim is precisely the destruction of man. This however is obviously our own species as perceived in others by each of its members in the context of scarcity.

> *Thus the human labour of the individual, and consequently, of the group is conditioned in its aim, and therefore in its movement, by man's fundamental project, for himself or for the group, of transcending scarcity, not only as the threat of death, but also as immediate suffering, and as the primitive relation which both constitutes Nature through man and constitutes man through Nature. But for precisely this reason scarcity will, without ceasing to be the fundamental relation, come to qualify the group or the individual who struggle against it by making themselves scarce so as to destroy it.*[218]

Sartre says that although on the one hand, scarcity gives

way to violence, but constructively scarcity can be occasion for the realignment of social groups also, with the project of combating it. It is seen that man makes his living in the midst of other men who are making theirs too, in the social field of scarcity. Now groups and institutions constitute and institutionalize themselves, insofar as scarcity is denied, in the unified field of the praxis, by labour. Labour defines itself necessarily, for man, as the praxis aiming to satisfy its need in the context of scarcity and by a special negation of the latter. All the environmental inertia in the way of praxis constitutes factors of scarcity.

He explains scarcity as the scarcity of the product, the scarcity of the tool, the scarcity of the worker, the scarcity of the consumer etc. There is double transition from scarcity under the influence of production itself. On the one hand there is transition from scarcity as the expendable character of each person with respect to all, to scarcity as society's designation of groups of under consuming producers [Here the relations becomes violence between groups].

On the other hand transition from absolute scarcity [where living together in a group in certain conditions is impossibility], to relative scarcity [as the impossibility, in given circumstances, for the group to grow beyond a certain limit without the mode or relations of production changing]. This relative scarcity passes into the rank of institution, in societies dividing into classes.

Matter

Worked matter can be seen in all its docility both as a new totalisation of society and its radical negation. In the moment of labour- the human moment in which man objectifies himself in producing his life, the inertia and material exteriority of objectification mean that, whatever else human relations may be, it is the product which defines men as others and constitutes them as another species, as anti-human; and that it is in the product that people produce their own objectivity, which returns to them as an enemy and constitutes them as other. Sartre quotes as such

> *Marx and many later thinkers have shown the meaning of these constraints of matter – how the iron and coal complex presents itself at the basis of a society as the condition for class mobility, for new functions and institutions, for more extreme differentiations and for changes in the system of property, etc. A new kind of men came into being, 'iron and coal men', produced by minning and by new smelting techniques, the industrial proletarians.*[219]

Inanimate matter is not defined by the actual substance of the particles composing it (which may be inert or living, inanimate or human), but by their relations among themselves and to the universe. We can also observe here, in this elementary form, the nature of reification. It is not a metamorphosis of the individual into a thing, as is often supposed but the necessity imposed by the structures of society on members of a social group, that they should live the fact that they belong, to the group and, thereby, to society as a whole, as a molecular statute. What they experience or do as individuals is still, immediately, real praxis or human labour. But a sort of mechanical rigidity haunts them in the concrete undertaking of living and subjects the result of their actions to the alien laws of totalising addition.

> *If materiality is everywhere and if it is linked to the meanings engraved in it by praxis, if a group of men can act as a quasi-mechanical system and a thing can produce its own idea, what becomes of matter, that is to say, Being totally without*

> *meaning? The answer is simple: it does not appear anywhere in human experience. At any moment of history things are human precisely to the extent that men are things. A volcanic eruption destroys Herculaneum; in a way, this is man destroying himself by the volcano. It is the social and material unity of the town and its inhabitants which, within the human world, confers the unity of an event on something which without men would perhaps dissolve into an indefinite process without meaning.*[220]

Sartre says that we situate man in the world and we simply note that for and through man this world cannot be anything but human. But the dialectic is precisely a form of monism, in that oppositions appear to it as moments which are posited for them for an instant before bursting. We always experience material reality as a threat to our lives, as resistance to our labour, as a limit to our knowledge and also as actual or possible instrumentality. But we experience it in society, where inertia, automatism and impenetrability act as a brake on our action, as well as in inert objects which resist our efforts. In both cases we experience this passive force within a process of signifying unification. Matter eludes us precisely to the extent that it is given to us and in us. The monism which starts from the human world and situates man in Nature is the monism of materiality. This is the only monism which is realist, and which removes the purely theological temptation to contemplate Nature, without alien addition.

> *It is the only monism which makes man neither a molecular dispersal nor a being apart, the only one which starts by defining him by his praxis in the general milieu of animal life, and which can transcend the following two true but*

> *contradictory propositions: all existence in the universe is material; everything in the world of man is human. But how can we ground praxis, the human relation of exteriority is based on the direct bond of interiority as the basic type of human relation. Man lives in a universe where the future is a thing, where the idea is an object and where the violence of matter is the 'Midwife of History'. But it is man who invests things with his own praxis, his own future and his own knowledge.*[221]

Man is precisely the material reality from which matter gets his human functions. In the indissoluble couple of 'matter' and 'human undertakings', each term modifies the other: the passive unity of the object determines material circumstances which the individual or the group transcend by their projects, that is by a real and active totalization aimed at changing the world.

Through the contradictions which it carries within it worked matter therefore becomes, by and for men, the fundamental motive force of history. In it the actions of all unite and take on a meaning, that is to say, they constitute for all the unity of a common future.

Necessity

Sartre gave good account of freedom which made man perfect and godlike, but in his later philosophy he explained one feature in man's life which is antagonistic to freedom which he calls necessity. At its most immediate level, dialectical investigation (*L'experience dialectique*) has emerged as praxis elucidating itself in order to control its own development. The certainty of this primary experience, in which doing granted its consciousness of itself, provides us with one certainty: it is reality itself which is revealed as presence to itself. The only concrete basis for the historical dialectic is the dialectical structure of individual action, which is embedded in the social milieu. Sartre has explained the dialectical intelligibility as the logic of practical totalisation and of real temporalisation. Men unwittingly realize their own unity in the form of antagonistic alterity through the material field in which they are dispersed and through the multiplicity of unifying actions which they perform upon this field.

> *I can see a group of people waiting for a bus, while none of them pays the slightest attention to the others, all eyes are turned the rue de Rennes, looking out for the bus which is about to arrive. In this state of semi-isolation, it is obvious that they are united by the street, the square, the paving stones and the asphalt, the pedestrian crossing and the bus, that is to say, by the material underside of a passivised praxis. Everything changes its sign when we enter the domain of the negative; from the point of view of this logic, the unity of men through matter can only be their separation. In other words, separation ceases to be a pure relation of exteriority and becomes a bond of lived interiority. People are separated by alterity by antagonisms, by their place in the system; but these separations, such as hatred, flight etc. are also modes of connection. However, since matter unites men in so far as it binds them together and forces them to enter a material system, it unifies them in so far as they are inertia.*[222a]

Dialectical intelligibility, however, is entirely preserved, since it enables one to grasp, in terms of the proliferation of acts, the type of negative unity represented by materiality. It is not that dialectic as idea produces exteriority as the reverse side of the idea: it is the real analytical dispersal of specifically dialectical agents, which they have to live as the interiorisation of exteriority. We understand that we have actually done something else and why our action has been altered outside us, we get our first dialectical experience of necessity.

> *Necessity appears in experience when we are robbed of our action by worked matter, not in so far as it is pure materiality but in so far as it is materialized praxis. In this moment, the tool made by another represents an element of exteriority in the dialectical field of interaction; but this exteriority does not derive from the external connections which are characteristics of inorganic materiality. All these connections are effectively taken up in the practical field of action. Exteriority exists to the extent that the tool as materiality is part of other fields of interiority. Finally, it is primarily a matter not of fields determined by the deliberate praxis of individuals or groups, but of the quasi-dialectical field whose fugitive unity does not come from anyone, but proceeds from matter to men who mediate between different sectors of materiality. In this way, a magical field of quasi-dialectical counter finality comes to be constituted: everything acts on everything else from a distance, and the slightest novelty produces complete devastation, just as if the material ensemble were a true totality. And the instrument used by given individual or community is transformed externally within the very hands which use it.*[222b]

The agent's real aim, and the agent himself, can only be assessed in the light of the result. It is necessary to recognize oneself as other in one's own individual objectification on the basis of another result. And this recognition is an experience of necessity because it shows us an unconstrained irreducibility inside the framework of intelligibility. The individual experience can occur only through the freedom of praxis. In other words, the basic experience of necessity is that of a retroactive power eroding my freedom, from the final objectivity to the original decision, but nevertheless emerging from it; it in the negation of freedom in the domain of complete freedom, sustained by freedom itself, and proportional. The man who can say both: "This is not what I wanted" and "I understand that this is what I have done and that I could not do anything else" and whose free praxis refers him to his prefabricated both – this man grasps, in an immediate dialectical movement, necessity as the destiny in exteriority of freedom.

We must recognise that the original relation between praxis as totalisation and materiality as passivity obliges man to objectify himself in a milieu which is not his own, and to treat an inorganic totality as his own objective reality. It is this relation between interiority and exteriority which originally constituted praxis as a relation of the organism to its material environment.

Social Being as Materiality – Class Being

After having understood the matter and necessity and its impact on human praxis we come to the point of social being. This social being is not dealt by Sartre in the sense of unification of individuals for common features of choice but underlying reality explains material ensemble and bjectification. He says that In the moment where we reach the apodictic structure of dialectical experience, still in its most abstract form, the discovery by the agent of the alienation of his praxis is accompanied by the discovery of his objectification as alienated. This means in fact that through a praxis which effaces itself before an inert, alienated objectivity, he discovers his being-outside-in-the-thing as his fundamental truth and his reality. And his being outside constitutes itself for him as practico-inert matter; either he himself, as a particularity, is roughly conditioned in exteriority by the whole universe, or, alternatively, his being awaits him from outside, prefabricated by a conjecture of exigencies.

> *At an elementary level of the social, everyone must become conscious of his being as the inorganic materiality of the outside interiorising itself in the form of a bond linking him to everyone else.*[223]

The individual enters into conflict with the situation in which he finds himself. But it is also true that all the actions he carries out as an individual merely reinforce and emphasis the objective being imposed on him: He quotes one example of a woman working in the Dop Shampoo factory, who has an abortion in order to avoid having a child she would be unable to feed, she makes a free decision in order to escape a destiny that is made for her; but this decision is itself completely manipulated by the objective situation: she realizes through herself what she is already; she carries out the sentence, which has already been passed on her, which deprives her of free motherhood. Being of the worker in a capitalist society is prefabricated by already performed, already crystallised labour. And his personal praxis, as a free productive dialectic, in turn transcends his prefabricated being by the very movement which it impresses on the lathe or machine-tool.

> *Inertia comes to him from the fact that previous work has constituted in the machine a future which cannot be transcended in the form of exigency and from the fact that this untranscendable future is*

> *actualised in all its urgency by present circumstances. Thus the inertia of praxis, as a new characteristics of it, removes none of its previous characteristics: praxis remains a transcendence of material being towards a future reorganisation of the field. And indeed it can always be said that any material circumstance which has to be transcended, even the configuration of the land in the course of a walk, imposes a certain content on the future towards which it is transcended. It restricts certain possibilities and provides a certain instrumentality which will characterize the final result. However it does not produce that future; the future comes to material circumstances through men.*[224]

We can now see why transcending one's class condition effectively means realising it. And since praxis, and the transparent movement of action, cannot alienate itself, we find different actions in everyone: one worker reads, another agitates, another finds time to do both, another has just bought a scooter, another plays the violin, and another does gardening. All these activities are constituted on the basis of particular circumstances, and they constitute the objective individuality of each person. But still in so far as they are located, in spite of themselves, inside a framework of exigencies that cannot be transcended, they simply realise everyone's class being.

Everyone makes himself signify by interiorising, by a free choice, the signification with which material exigencies have produced him as a signified being. Class-being, as practico-inert being mediated by the passive synthesis of worked matter, comes to men through men; for each of us it is our being outside ourselves in matter, in so far as this produces us and awaits us from birth and in so far as it constitutes itself through us as a future fatality, that is to say as a future which will necessarily realise itself through us, through the otherwise arbitrary actions which we choose. It is obvious that this class-being does not prevent us from realising an individual destiny, but this realisation of our experience until death is only one of several possible ways (determined by the structured field of possibilities) of producing our class being. It will be appropriate to show that they can be organised only on the basis of inert structures representing both a qualification of their action and its objective limit, including its secret inertia.

Individuals realize their class structures through one another: from elementary praxis, from working in a workshop, everyone's class-being, in so far as it is a practico-inert exigency of machines, comes to him not only from the class which exploits him, but also from all his comrades; or rather, it comes to him from the class which exploits him and the machines which require him through the medium of his comrades and their universal character as exploited.

Class-being defines itself for everyone as an inert (untranscendables) relation with his class comrades on the basis of certain structures. Destiny, general (and even particular) Interest, Exigency, Class Structures, Value as common limits, all necessarily direct our attention not only to a type of individual being which we have already described, but also, through it, to a type of collective being as the basis of all individual reality. It refers to inert collective being, as the inorganic common materiality of all the members of a given ensemble. For the term does not primarily mean either the active unification of all the individuals within the organization which they themselves have produced, or an identity of nature between several separate products.

Collective Structures

Social objects (collective structures) are, at least in their fundamental structure, beings of the practico-inert field. Their being therefore resides in inorganic materiality in so far as, in this field, it is itself practico-inert. These are practical realities with their existences to the extent that they realise in and through themselves the interpretation of a multiplicity of unorganised individuals within them and they produce every individual in them in the indistinction of a totality.

The Series:

The first one is the series which has been explained by Sartre with an example of people grouped around the same but stop. These individuals form a group in that they have a common interest. Separated as organic individuals, structure of their practico-inert is common to them and unifies them from without. It is simple identity, designating the user as a distract generality by a definite praxis (signal the bus, climb aboard, pay the fare and sit down).

> *Take a grouping of people in the place Saint-Germain. They are waiting for a bus at a bus stop in front of the church. These people – who may differ greatly in age, sex, class and social milieu – realise, within the ordinariness of everyday life, the relation of isolation, of reciprocity and of unification from outside which is characteristics of, for example the residents of a big city in so far as they are united though not integrated through work, through struggle or through any other activity in an organised group common to them all. These people do not care about or speak to each other and, in general, they do not look at one another, they exist side by side alongside a bus stop. In our example, isolation becomes, for and through everyone, for him and for others, the real, social product of cities. For each members of the group waiting for the bus, the city is in fact present as the practico-inert ensemble. No one*

> *helps anyone; it's every man for himself'. The city has been there since morning, as requirement, as instrumentality, as social milieu etc. And, through the medium of the city, there are given the millions of people who are the city and whose completely invisible presence makes of everyone both a polyvalent isolation (with millions of facets). And at the same time integrated member of the city.*[225]

Isolation is a project. It is relative to certain individuals and to certain moments : to isolate oneself by reading the paper is to utilize the national collectivity and in the end, the totality of living men, insofar as one figures among them and is dependent on all of them.

The relation of reciprocity remains in the gathering itself, and among its members; the negation of isolation by praxis preserves it as negated: it is, in fact, quite simply, the practical existence of men among men. Not only is there a lived reality – for everyone even if he turns his back on others, and is unaware of their number and their appearance, knows that they exist as a finite and indeterminate plurality of which he is a part – but also, even outside everyone's real relation to the others, the ensemble of isolated behaviour, in so far as it is conditioned by historical totalisation, presupposes a structure of reciprocity at every level. This reciprocity must be the most constant possibility and the most immediate reality, for otherwise the social models in currency (clothes, hair style, bearing etc.) would not be adopted by everyone and neither would everyone hasten to repair anything wrong with their dress as soon as they notice it, and if possible in secret. This shows that isolation does not remove one from the visual and practical field of the other, and that it realises itself objectively in this field.

These individuals form a group to the extent that they

have a common interest, so that, though separated as organic individuals, they share a structure of their practico-inert being, and it unites them from outside. They are all regular users of the bus service: they know the time-table and frequency of the buses and consequently they all wait for the same bus. This object, in so far as they are dependent upon it (breakdowns, failures, accidents), is their present interest. The bus they wait for unites them, it is their interest as commuters; everything is temporalised: the traveller recognises himself as a resident, and then the bus becomes characterised by its daily eternal return. The object takes on a structure which overflows its pure inert existence; as such it is provided with a passive future and part and these make it appear to the passengers as a fragment of their destiny.

The moment must be regarded, quite simply, as the abstract stage of identity. Insofar as they have the same reality in future (a moment longer, the same moment for all, and the vehicle will appear around the corner), the unjustifiable separation of these organisms (insofar as it arises from other conditions and another regions of being) is determined as identity.

> *There is identity when the common interest is revealed, and when the plurality is defined exactly with respect to that interest. The identity of each person with each other is their unity over there, as being-other; here and now, it is their common alterity.*[226]

At this level the material object will determine the serial order as the social reason for the separation of individuals. The practico-inert requirement emerges, here out of scarcity: there is not enough room for everyone, the number of people in proportion to the number of seats – would designate without any particular practical arrangement, each person as in excess.

> *The travellers waiting for the bus take tickets indicating the order of their arrival. This means that they accept the impossibility of deciding which individuals are dispensable in terms of the intrinsic qualities of the individuals; in other words, that they remain on the terrain of common interest. Serial unity, as common interest, therefore imposes itself as exigency and destroys all opposition. The fact of having arrived first does not give any distinctive characteristics, but simply the right to get on the bus first.*[227]

There are social behaviour, serial feelings and serial thoughts; in other words a series is made of being for individuals both in relation to one another and in relation to their common being and this mode of being transforms all their structures. In every non-serial praxis, a serial praxis will be found, as the practico-inert structure of the praxis in so far as it is social.

Collectives [Indirect Gatherings]:

Indirect gatherings explain rationality of alterity as a rule of the social practico-inert field. Sartre says that In accordance with their own structure and passive action, practico-inert objects produce the gathering as a direct or indirect relation between the members of the multiplicity. The relation based on presence will be referred to as direct. Housewives queering in front of a baker's shop, in a period of shortage, are characterized as a gathering with a serial structure; and this gathering is direct: the possibility of a sudden unitary praxis (a riot) is immediately given. On the other hand, these can be practico-inert objects whose structure is completely determinate but which, within the indeterminate multiplicity of men (of a city, a nation, or the world), themselves constitute a given plurality as an indirect gathering. And I define such gatherings by absence; by which I mean not so much absolute distance which is, in reality only an abstraction, as the impossibility of individuals establishing relations of reciprocity between themselves or a common praxis, in so far as they are defined by this object as members of the gatherings.

> *The mere fact of listening to the radio, that is to say; of listening to a particular broadcast at a particular time, establishes a serial relation of absence between the different listeners. In this way, the practico-inert object not only produces a unity of individuals outside themselves in inorganic matter, but also determines them in separation and, in so far as they are separate, ensures their communication through alterity.*[228]

The practico-inert field exists, that it is real, and the free human activities are not thereby eliminated, that they are not even altered in their translucidity as projects in the process of being realised. The field exists: in short, it is what surrounds and conditions us. I need only glance out of the window: I will be able to see cars which are men and drivers who are cars, a policeman who is directing the traffic at the corner of the street and a little further on, the same traffic being controlled by red and green lights: hundreds of exigencies rise up towards me: pedestrian crossings, notices and prohibitions; collectives (a cafe, a church); and instruments (a taxi rank, a bus stop etc.). These beings neither thing nor man, but practical unites made up of man and inert things: these appeal and these exigencies do not yet concern me directly. Later I will go down into the street and become their thing.

Alienation:

This structure explains that the person is not able to live with the truth within him, the truth which could make him a true individual, but living as an objective human he feels alienated. Sartre explains it as such:

> *To be alienated or simply altered, the individual must be an organism susceptible of dialectical action and it is through the free praxis that necessity is revealed as a transformation of his product and himself by his product in the other. His praxis reveals all this to him, and interiorizes them. His free activity, in its freedom, takes upon itself everything that crushes him. Exhausting work, exploitation, oppression, rising prices.*[229]

Here we have one example. The semiautomatic machine dreams through the women workers, lost in some day dream and moving in a rhythm external to them – which is everyone's work itself as other and as for this rhythm, which is so alien to the personal rhythms of her life that for the first few days it seemed absolutely unendurable: the woman worker wanted to adapt herself to it, she made an effort. The total adaptation to semi-automation meant the destruction of her bodily rhythms and the interiorisation of a rhythm which was absolutely other. But the moment in which the girl emerged as the object of the machine – that is to say, when mystification revealed itself in objective alienation was also the moment in which her adaptation was accomplished.

In other words freedom in this context, does not mean the possibility of choice but the necessity of living these constraints in the form of exigencies which must be fulfilled by a praxis. The family situation (the illness or unemployment of some of its members) may constitute itself in the practico-inert field, as the impossibility of ensuring the survival of all its members unless a particular woman or old man resumes work.Here this alienation of individual shows strength of matter, as the individual by constituting itself exhausts itself by surrendering its own sovereignty to this piece of matter. As matter cannot be transcended, its inertia alters the praxis.

It would be wrong to interpret me as saying that man is free in all situations, as the stoics claimed. I mean the exact opposite: all men are slaves in so far as their life unfolds in the practico-inert field and in so far as this field is always conditioned by scarcity.

Groups:

Groups always constitute themselves on the basis of certain particular contradictions which define a particular sector of the field of passive activity, while one cannot have any a priori assurance that the same applies everywhere. When such contradictions occur, then, as we shall see, the dialectical praxis of the individual puts itself on trial at the heart of the anti-dialectic which appropriates its results, and inverts itself in another social space as the totalisation of multiple actions in, for and by a totalising objective result. Men totalise, and totalise themselves, in order to reorganise themselves into the unity of a praxis: that which totalises the human world in the historical undertaking. This new structure of the investigation presents itself as an inversion of the practico-inert field: that is to say, the nerve of practical unity is freedom, appearing as the necessity of necessity, in other words, as its inexorable inversion. Indeed, in so far as the individuals in a given milieu are directly threatened, in practico-inert necessity, by the impossibility of life, their radical unity is the inflexible negation of this impossibility (To live working or die fighting); thus the group constitutes itself as the radical impossibility of living, which threatens serial multiplicity. But this new dialectic, in which freedom and necessity are now one is not a new incarnation of the transcendental dialectic: It is a human construction whose sole agents are individual men as free activities.

This structure denotes collectivity of individuals practicing a common praxis. This upheaval originates in a synthetic and material transformation, occurring in the context of scarcity and of existing structures.

> *The origin of any restructuring of collectivity into group is a complex fact that occurs simultaneously at every stage of materiality, but a fact that is transcended, as organizing praxis, at the level of serial unity.*[230]

As far as the constitution of a group is concerned we find ourselves in a vicious circle. The fused group constitute itself on the basis of a need or common danger and defines itself by the common objective which determines its common praxis. Yet neither common need, nor common praxis, nor common objective can define a community unless it makes itself into a community by feeling individual need as common need, and by projecting itself, in the internal unification of a common integration, towards objectives which it produces as common. The common object, as the unity of the multiple outside itself is above all the producer of serial unity and that it is on the basis of this double determination that the anti-dialectical structure of the collectivity or alterity constitutes itself.

It is a ternary relation. Indeed, this is something that no picture or sculpture could convey directly, in that the individual, as a third party, is connected, in the unity of a single praxis, with the unity of individuals as inseparable moments of a non-totalised totalisation, and with each of them as a third party, that is to say, through the mediation of the group. The members of the group are third parties, which means that each of them totalises them reciprocities of others. And the relation of one third party to another has nothing to do with alterity: since the group is the practical milieu of this relation, it must be a human relation, which we shall call mediated reciprocity.

> *The basis of intelligibility, for the fused group, is that the structure of certain objectives is revealed through the praxis of the individual as demanding*

> *the common unity of a praxis which is everyone's. The structure of synthetic unity is, therefore, even at the level of the univocal relation of interiority directly derived from the grasp of a unitary (and passive) structure of the surrounding materiality through the synthetic unity of a dialectical, individual praxis.*[231]

At this level there is group behaviour and there are group thoughts in that the common praxis is self-elucidating: and the essential structure of these practical thoughts is the unveiling of the world as a new reality through a negation of the old world as a new reality through a negation of the old reality of impotence, that is to say, through the negation of the impossibility of humanity. The fact that the origin of the grouping was terror is not actually very significant; every praxis constitutes itself as an opening made in the future and sovereignly affirms its own possibility simply through the emergence of the undertaking itself, that is to say, it makes success into a structure of practical freedom.

Terror:

The basis of terror is the fact that the group has not and cannot have the ontological status that it claims in its praxis; conversely it is the fact that each and every person is produced and defined on the basis of this non-existent totality. This negative factor, serves as a reinforcement of the group. As Sartre says:

> *There is a sort of interior emptiness, an indeterminate and unbridgeable distance of uneasiness in each community, large or small; this uneasiness gives rise to a reinforcement of the practices of integration and increases proportionately with the increased integration of the group.*[232]

The group has two negations, the individual praxis and the sociality. Group was formed in opposition to this seriality. It is individual praxis which constitutes the suspect for the apparatus of terror. It is realized by deliberations and decisions that themselves create recurrence and at the same time by processes that are realized in the tension of transcendence – immanence.

Terror arises out of opposition to seriality and not freedom. It is freedom liquidating, by means of violence, the indefinite flight of the other that is powerlessness.

The Institution:

The institution has contradictory characteristics of being both praxis and a thing. Institution is a carcass, and those who are institutionalized have a real comprehension of the institution's end. Institution possesses a considerable force of inertia because it posits itself, by and in its inert-being, as essentiality, defining men as the inessential means of its perpetuation.

Sartre explains that institution is fundamentally unchangeable. It is because individual's praxis is determined in the institutionalized group as incapable of changing the institution. And this powerlessness is originated in one's relation of circular otherness with the other members of the group.

> *The unity of the institution is the unity of the otherness insofar as it is introduced into the group and insofar as it is used by the group to replace its own missing unity.*[233]

The moment of common degradation at which the institution appears is precisely that in which each person claims to reject freedom for himself, in order to realize, as a thing, the imperial unity of the descending group.

Chapter-5
Concluding Sartre's Concept of Man

Summary of the Book

Sartre is one of the best known philosophers of the 20th Century from France. The central theme of his philosophy is atheistic and goes with the dictum that 'Existence precedes Essence'. He explains that in man and man alone, existence precedes essence. Sartre used different terms as mankind, human-reality, human being and the for-itself (*pour-soi*) with the same meaning. His explanation is logical in the sense that it is based on concrete facts, so Sartre calls it phenomenological ontology. He explained detailed analysis of the absolute freedom of man and its implication for humanism as well as man caught up in economic necessities and formation of social man as a result of need, scarcity and necessity.

The first chapter 'Man as Being and Nothingness' explains man in terms of Being and nothingness arising out of it. Explanation of Being rejects dualism of appearance and reality which says that appearances refer to the total series of appearances and not to a hidden reality which would drain to itself all the being of the existent. Phenomenon is what manifests itself. Being manifests itself to all in some way, all the phenomena taken by the appearance indicate towards the being. The world on the whole is the Being. There are two absolutely separated regions of being.

1. *The being of the pre-reflective cogito – Being-for-itself.*
2. *The being of the phenomenon – Being-in-itself.*

Sartre explains consciousness as pre-reflective cogito and as the being of the percipere. Consciousness is the knowing being in his capacity as being and not as being known. We come into contact with consciousness as a basic existence which makes man a man, and not an object in the world. Sartre explains consciousness as the transcending for-itself. He says that Consciousness is a being such that in its being, it's being is in question, in so far as this being implies a being other than itself. It is of two types:

1. Unreflective consciousness, also called non-thetic consciousness or non-positional self-consciousness. This is the pre-reflective cogito.
2. Reflective consciousness [also called thetic consciousness or positional self-consciousness].

Consciousness is a being, whose existence posits its essence, and inversely it is consciousness of a being, whose essence implies its existence; that is, in which appearance lays claim to being. The other part of the being which is non-living is termed as being-in-itself. No argument supports origin of being-in-itself. Being is itself. It is an immanence which cannot realize itself, it is glued to itself. Being is in-itself. It is beyond becoming. It encompasses no negation, it is full positivity. Thus being-in-itself is called contingent. Sartre explains three characteristics of being-in-itself:

> *1. Being is. 2. Being is in-itself. 3. Being is what it is.*

The connection between two regions of Being is Nothingness. Being and Nothingness are two complementary components of the real, which are united somehow in the production of existents. Nothingness is subsequent to being as it is being which is first posited then denied. The in-itself being full positivity cannot be origin of nothingness, so the reason is an active being, that is the for-itself. So the Being who nihilates nothingness in its being should be its own nothingness, connected with its own being. This being has appeared to us as freedom. Human freedom precedes essence in man and makes it possible. This freedom to choose action is the heaviness on man's being which is called anguish. When one recognizes one's possibility, as one's possibility only, anguish is born as there is no excuse to escape from it.

The second chapter 'The Human Reality' is concerned with the for-itself, the others and concrete relations in the world. All the concepts, such as consciousness, nothingness, the being-in-itself are merged within the concept of being-for-itself. The for-itself is 'Man'. The nothingness which arises in the heart of consciousness that is man: is not, it is made to be, thus nothingness is not possible in the non-reflective cogito because nothingness is always an elsewhere. The for-itself never exists except in the form of an elsewhere in relation to itself. Anguish aroused out of nothingness gives way to two modes of conduct. One is freedom and the other is 'Bad faith'. A bad faith is a lie to oneself within the unity of single consciousness, wherein one denies one's total freedom and chooses to behave as an inert object or start believing in determinism. It is self-deception. Bad-faith is not to expel anguish but to surpass the nothingness which a man is in relation to himself. Presence of man in the world makes him realize that he is in a situation. This presents facticity to the for-itself in the form of in-itself. This in-itself, remains at the heart of the for-itself as its original contingency. One more important aspect related to the life of man is desire. Existence of desire as a human fact is sufficient to prove that human reality is a lack. The self as being-in-itself is what human reality lacks and it gives meaning to human reality. The for-itself lacks the self or itself as in-itself. The being of the self is value. So human-reality is that by which value arises in the world and possibilities arise out of lack of human-reality. These possibilities make relation between the for-itself and the world. Sartre used the expression circuit of selfness to explain this relation. Structure of nothingness explains that the human reality is temporal. Temporality is an organized structure of three 'elements' – the past, the present and the future and meaning of the for-itself's transcendence lies in temporality. Sartre explains one more mode of consciousness within reflective description; the 'Others'. He uses an example of 'shame' to explain it. Shame recognizes the existence of the other perceiving me when I am in an awkward position. The other appears to me empirically through the perception of a body and this body is an in-itself external to my body. So this relation which unites and separates our bodies is a spatial relation, the relation of things which have no relation among themselves. The for-itself recognizes the other for-itself through his look. Sartre says that If my look grants me my subjectivity then his look grants him his subjectivity, with my permanent possibility of being seen by the other as an object. The body explains an important fact of the for-itself. The body individualizes the for-itself. The body is a concrete presence of the for-itself in the world. Thus the for-itself is both body and consciousness. The for-itself is a relation to the world, so for human-reality, to be is to-be-there. It is an ontological necessity. The body is an instrument which is utilized with other instruments. The same is true for other's body. Concrete relations are relations between individuals as well as among groups. Two basic dimensions are love and hate. The love recognizes freedom while hate is failure of love as well as failure of all the relations which arise in between frequencies of love and hate.

The third chapter 'Freedom of Man' includes concept of freedom arising out of ontological study of man as well as psychological investigation through the free human projects to assert the fundamental Being. It also includes implications of ontology, the free man bound to social structures as a social being and concluding vision of Sartre's man. The freedom is an essence of the life of the for-itself. This freedom becomes explicit through the acts of man. He says that human reality is free because it is not enough. It is free because it is perpetually wrenched away from itself and because it has been separated by a nothingness from what it is and from what it will be. The fundamental act of freedom is to choose oneself. Our choice is always a conscious choice. All choices refer to the fundamental choice or original choice. Fundamental project means man's total being-in-the-world. The freedom reveals facticity to the for-itself. The facticity which is in-itself is revealed and utilized by the for-itself. On the one hand it helps the for-itself to authenticate its existence and on the other hand creates obstacle in way of the for-itself to exercise its freedom to achieve the desired end. For Sartre freedom being absolute for man, the man carries the weight of the whole world on his shoulders. He is responsible for the world and for himself as a way of being. The peculiar character of human-reality is that it is without excuse. Original project of the man is the project of being. Human reality is the desire of being the foundation of its own being-in-itself, which can be called God. Thus man is the being whose project is to be God. This fundamental project is everywhere in all desires. Sartre suggests an enquiry through the concrete projects of man to understand the being of man. A specific method for this is called existential psychoanalysis. It seeks to determine the original choice. It can be known through possessions of man. We desire to possess this object or to do that thing or to be someone. Thus it can be said that desire of a particular object means the desire to be united with it in an internal relation, it is determination of the being. On the bases of the study so far Sartre tries to answer the metaphysical implications of his ontology. The metaphysical question raises a matter of 'why' in terms of being. He says that the question is devoid of meaning as all the 'whys' in fact are subsequent to being and presuppose it. Being is, without cause and without necessity; the being releases to us its original contingency. There is being because the for-itself is such that there is being and the characteristics of phenomenon comes to being through the for-itself itself. Although the for-itself seems to be shut up within himself but his absolute freedom and his relation with others, describes him as an ethical being. The ethical implications of phenomenological ontology are what Sartre describes as humanism. He says that existentialism is a humanism. Nonexistence of the creator in his philosophy demands for someone to invent values and to have a sense of responsibility. Although decisions are purely subjective but area of responsibility is not limited to subjective level, for it concerns mankind as a whole. This is humanism, because we find that there is no legislator but himself; that he himself, thus abandoned, must decide for himself.

In the fourth chapter, 'Man as a Social Being' he defined his man in relation to social structure and economic terms under the influence of Marxism. Practically man, faces the world with real problems. This real man is discoverable in need, this is the first totalizing relation between that material being, a man and the material group to which he belongs. Man as a living totality, satisfies its needs in the surrounding materiality. The factor of scarcity is revealed when man judges the material environment in terms of need. Each of them is a threat to his life. For each person, man exists as inhuman man, as an alien species. Human relations (positive or negative) are relations of reciprocity; without this human relation of reciprocity, the inhuman relation of scarcity would not exist. We always experience material reality as a threat to our lives, as resistance to our labour, as a limit to our knowledge and also as actual or possible instrumentality. The monism which starts from the human world and situates man in Nature is the monism of materiality. This is the only monism which is realist, and which removes the purely theological temptation to contemplate Nature, without alien addition. Man is precisely the material reality from which matter gets his human functions. In the indissoluble couple of 'matter' and human undertakings', each term modifies the other. We understand that we have actually done something else and why our actions have been altered outside us, we get our first dialectical experience of necessity. The basic experience of necessity is that of a retroactive power eroding my freedom. The man grasps, in an immediate dialectical movement, necessity as the destiny in exteriority of freedom. A lot of social structures arise in this practical world of need and scarcity. One of them is 'solitude'. It is in fact the pure and simple practical existence of men among men. One more structure is the series. Sartre explains it with an example of people grouped around the same but stop. The important structural explanation is alienation. Sartre explains it through an example of girls working in the factory. The group is a structure which denotes collectivity of individuals practicing a common praxis. What defines a community is the feeling of individual need as common need, towards the objectives that it produces as common. Social structure of terror arises out of opposition to seriality and it is not freedom. It is freedom liquidating, by means of violence, the indefinite flight of the other that is powerlessness.

Sartre's vision of man can be concluded as that of ontologically free man and socially relative man. In other words man is a subjective consciousness but objective human being. Man finds his authenticity in humanism, which is based on the subjective efforts and goes to the objective. What the man needs is to find himself again and to understand that nothing can save him from himself, not even a valid proof of the existence of God. In this sense existentialism is optimistic; it is a doctrine of action.

Conclusion

Jean Paul Sartre a great philosopher of 20th century established new dimentions of thought and method in existentialism. We can see freshness, logic, creativity and daring spirit in his ideas. The most interesting factor in his philosophy is acceptance of change in his own ideas although basic concepts of existentialism were carried throughout life, even then changing scenario of the world and new demands of time were adjusted with logic and honesty. Sartre's vision of man goes on two platforms. His earlier philosophy presents an account of perfect life of man in his subjectivity and freedom but in later stage the reality overpowers in a different manner where need, hunger, scarcity, matter, formation of groups and societies brings a kind of objectivity in the life of man. Thus his man comes out as an ontologically free man and socially relative man. As a philosopher this change can be appreciated as he himself understood and accepted the change. In his autobiography, *The Words,* he said that, "He had experienced reality and seen children dying of hunger. Nausea diminishes in importance at the sight of a dying child." When Sartre says that man is condemned to be free, it is according to the ontological conclusion of the for-itself. This for-itself who is a man exercises his freedom against every obstacle. This freedom, for man is a subjective experience in the objective world. This freedom is absolute as there is no God to help him take decisions. Man accepts what is given to him and manipulate it to achieve the kind of being he wants himself to be and this manipulation is kind of caressing of in-itself and Others. It is similar to the saying of Dr. Radhakrishnan, that take the life as a card game, in which only the given cards can be used to play the game, whether you win or lose depends on the way you play with them. Becoming factor in the ontological being of man makes him realize his absolute freedom. But in the description of social man freedom is taken over by its antagonistic which is 'necessity'. This necessity explains need and scarcity in the life of man and hurdles created by material things of the world. Man becomes helpless and his freedom is confined to choose from the given sources. Man feels a sort of alienation. This alienation is described as dual character of man where inner aspirations and dreams are suppressed in the face of external demands and the man starts believing this external being as his real self. Alienation of individual shows strength of matter, as the individual by constituting itself exhausts itself by surrendering its own sovereignty to this piece of matter. As matter cannot be transcended, its inertia alters the praxis.

Sartre says that Being of man is related to his original choice. This original choice of man is related to the desire of man. Desire, resides neither in the outside world nor in consciousness. It is a way by which consciousness relates itself to objects of the world. He says that I exist as truly human only in going beyond my immediate being in pursuit of an aim which is not dictated to me but which I freely project. Becoming process of man explains the reason in the lack. Thus human reality is a lack and it desires to fill this lack, to become a complete self. This completion it finds in the in-itself only, thus man desires to be for-itself-in-itself, that is God. Sartre's desire leads only to a non-existent ideal which is basically self-contradictory and irrational.

> *To be man means to reach towards being God. Or if you prefer, man fundamentally is the desire to be God...every human reality is a passion in that it projects losing itself so as to found being and by the same stroke to stroke to constitute the in-itself which escapes contingency by being its own foundation, the 'Ens Causa Sui', which religions calls God.*[234]

Every action of man is an act of freedom, even his useless passion to be a God for himself is an act of freedom and when he feels anguish and tries to find solace in determinism or when he stops to believe about himself that he is an in-itself, both are acts of freedom. But believing to be an in-itself or to believe in God is bad-faith. For theistic theories to believe in God is faith but he calls it bad-faith.

He says that ontologically man's being is such that metaphysical questions or answers do not fit into its structure. Man can answer 'what' but cannot answer 'why' about being. Thus it is comfortable and intelligible to be in the limit of one's capability. In this regard he has been compared to Buddha by Kaufmann.

> *Nevertheless, the Buddha, too, opposed any reliance on the divine because he wanted men to realize their complete responsibility. His final, and perhaps most characteristic, words, according to tradition were: "Work out your own salvation with diligence." And if the diligence is rather uncharacteristic of the existentialists, the Buddha's still more radical dictum with which the Dhammapada opens is nothing less than the quintessence of Sartre's thought: "All that we are is the result of what we have thought." Few words in world literature equal the impact of this saying. All man's alibis are unacceptable: no gods are responsible for his condition; no heredity and no environment.*[235]

Freedom is not only contemplation but action. Upsurge of the for-itself in the world and his relation to the world, both things are possible in action only. Every choice, decision and act is subjective as man cannot be otherwise but a subjective being.

Man connects to the world on two levels; the first connection is between the for-itself and the in-itself. He is surrounded by in-itself from all directions. The past, the future, the objects of the world, facticity, everything presents an in-itself to him. All the possessions he does throughout life are also called the in-itself, whether they are objects or achievements or artistic creations. In this way the in-itself helps him to rise up in the world as the for-itself. The second connection is between the for-itself and the Others in the sphere of humanity. One man understands the other through acts thus it is essential that the choice should be right as it will affect other men. Thus man is responsible for whatever he does. This man to man relation of responsibility is humanity in Sartre's words.

> *Am I really a man.who has the right to act in such a manner that humanity regulates itself by what I do.*[236]

Atheistic existentialism says that 'existence is prior to essence', and this places man in a position as a creator of values as Sartre denies existence of every kind of eternal idea and objective value thus humanity based on abstract principles is not acceptable to him. Consistent atheism requires the denial of objective values and supports man as a subjective being, and creator of values.

> *Our aim is precisely to establish the human kingdom as a pattern of values in distinction from the material world. But the subjectivity which we thus postulate as the standard of truth is no narrowly individual subjectivism, for as we have*

> *demonstrated, it is not only one's own self that one discovers in the cogito, but those of others too.*[237]

Here we find a little drift in his philosophy of later stage. The in-itself which initially caused physical and philosophical nausea in his novel *Nausea,* became a positivity in *Being and Nothingness* as a cause of values and aspirations in man and finally came out as a reason of necessity, alienation, terror and violence in the form of external materiality. He says that all men are slaves in so far as their life unfolds in the practico-inert field and in so far as this field is always conditioned by scarcity. But further he says that all existence in the universe is material; everything in the world of man is human. It is man who invests things with his own praxis, his own future and his own knowledge.

Sartre's conclusion of ontological description of man seemed a failure or pessimism in Being and Nothingness as he said that 'man is a useless passion', thus depicting failure of man in terms of end and in The Critique of Dialectical Reason, he came out as a man less strong than initial one in terms of matter but implications of his ontology in humanism mend every loophole as man has been explained as an absolute being and as well as socially relative person. Here we have a concept of 'should be' which explains that what is perfect and right never compromises on hurdles. It means free, responsible man decides humanity in his subjectivity. Man is responsible for what he is. Existentialism is a doctrine which affirms that every truth and every action imply both an environment and a human subjectivity.

Although ontological description of man as the for-itself seems to be shut up within himself but his absolute freedom and his relation with others, describes him as an ethical being. The ethical implications of phenomenological ontology are what Sartre describes as humanism.

Ultimately Sartre calls his philosophy as 'existentialism is humanism'.

Sense of responsibility makes man a man. Although every man's decisions are purely subjective but area of responsibility is not limited to subjective level as it expands toward whole mankind. Sartre says that man is not only responsible for his individuality, but for all men.

> *When we say that man chooses himself, we do mean that everyone of us must choose himself; but that we also mean that in choosing for himself he chooses for all men.*[238]

To choose between this or that is at the same time to affirm the value of that which is chosen; for man is unable to choose the worse. What we choose is always better for all and nothing can be better for us unless it is better for all. So responsibility carries much greater meaning, for it concerns mankind as a whole. I am hereby committing not only myself, but humanity as a whole. In this sense I am creating a certain image of man as I would have him to be. According to Sartre in fashioning myself I fashion man.

Ethical implications explain ethical and social man moving from subjective values to objective values. As humanism explains ethical, Sartre's humanism is based on subjective efforts and goes to the objective. The meaning is simple, we are free, therefore we choose, that is to say, we invent. There are no rules of general morality to show us what we ought to do: no signs are vouchsafed in this world.

Ontological explanation explains that we are just as certain of the other as we are of ourselves. Thus the man who discovers himself directly in the cogito also discovers all the others, and discovers them as the condition of his own existence. Thus, at once, man finds him in a world which is that of inter-subjectivity. This inter-subjectivity tells that every purpose, however individual it may be, is of universal value.

> *Every purpose, even that of a Chinese, of an Indian or of a Negro, can be understood by a European. In this sense we may say that there is a human universality, but it is not something given; it is being perpetually made. I make this universality in choosing myself; I also make it by understanding the purpose of any other man, of whatever epoch. This absoluteness of the act of choice does not alter the relativity of each epoch.*[239]

Sartre says that reality means sum of appearances, in this way man is a totality, described through sum of his actions. Ontological description of the for-itself explains that man is a perpetual striving toward the end or purpose. Man is never complete.

> *An existentialist will never take man as the end, since man is still to be determined and we have no right to believe that humanity is something to which we could set up a cult.*[240]

Man is all the time outside of himself: it is in projecting and losing himself beyond himself that he makes man to exist; and, on the other hand, it is by pursuing transcendent aims that he himself is able to exist.

Sartre's existentialism is not atheist in the sense that it would exhaust itself in demonstrations of the non-existence of God. It declares that even if God existed that would make no difference from its point of view. But we think that the real problem is not that of God's existence; what man needs is to find himself again and to understand that nothing can save him from himself, not even a valid proof of the existence of God. In this sense existentialism is optimistic; it is a doctrine of action

So it is existent man who questions anything and we cannot find any proof of God from this human existence. It is man all alone who decides about himself practically in his freedom. Going on these lines it is impossible to prove existence of God, thus he discards the idea of God from man's existence. We can mention about the Denish philosopher Soren Kierkegaard who was against rational approach when a question related to existence of God was to be answered. Kierkegaard believed that only passion and feelings can help us to reach the truth. He was a strong advocate of the concept of faith. He said that to believe or have faith in God is to know that one has no perpetual or any other access to God, and yet still has faith in God. On Kierkegaard's religious views, Sartre offers this argument against existence of God: If existence precedes essence, it follows from the meaning of the term sentient that a sentient being cannot be complete or perfect. [In *Being and Nothingness*, Sartre's phrasing is that God would be a *pour-soi* (a being-for-itself; a consciousness) who is also an *en-soi* (a being-in-itself; a thing): which is a contradiction in terms]. Sartre agrees with Kierkegaard's analysis of Abraham undergoing anxiety (Sartre calls it anguish), but Sartre doesn't agree that God told him to do it. In his lecture, *Existentialism is a Humanism*, he says that The man who lies in self-excuse, by saying, "Everyone will not do it" must be ill at ease in his conscience, for the act of lying implies the universal value which it denies. By its very disguise his anguish reveals itself. This is the anguish that Kierkegaard called "the anguish of Abraham." You know the story: An angel commanded Abraham, to sacrifice his son; and obedience was obligatory, if it really was an angel who had appeared and said, "Thou, Abraham, shalt sacrifice thy son." But anyone in such a case would wonder, first, whether it was indeed an angel and secondly, whether I am really Abraham. Where are the proofs? A certain mad woman who suffered from hallucinations said that people were telephoning to her, and giving her orders. The doctor asked, "But who is it that speaks to you?" She replied: "He says it is God." And what, indeed, could prove to her that it was God? If an angel appears to me, what is the proof that it is an angel; or, if hear voices, who can prove that they proceed from heaven and not from hell, or from my own sub-consciousness or some pathological condition? Who can prove that they are really addressed to me?

Sartre's bad-faith which is absolutely against, what Kierkegaard calls faith in God. Sartre says that when man is not feeling oneself ready up to the demands of future responsibility he feels anguish and seeks escape and this escape leads one to the bad-faith, that is faith is determinism or in any super power. According to Sartre man is on the wrong track and his way in unauthentic, a weak way in fact. Sartre's God is self-sufficient, capable, strong man who lives authentic human life, like a confident person.

Jean Paul Sartre a great philosopher is a milestone in the field of philosophy. He is a guide to those who can think, decide and move ahead.

References

1. Jean-Paul Sartre, *A propos de l' existentialisme: mise au point*, Action Magazine, December 29, 1944
2. Jean-Paul Sartre, *Existentialism*, Translated by Bernard Frechtman (Philosophical Library, New York, 1947), p. 50.
3. Jean-Paul Sartre, *The Words – The Autobiography of Jean-Paul Sartre*, Translated by Bernard Frechtman (Vintage Books, New York, 1964).
4. Jean-Paul Sartre, *The Transcendence of the Ego*, Translated by Forest Williams and Robert Kirkpatrick (Noonday, New York, 1957), p. 111.
5. Ibid., p. 120.
6. Jean-Paul Sartre, *Nausea*, Translated by Robert Baldick (Penguin Books Ltd., London, 1963), p. 18.
7. Ibid., p. 22.
8. Ibid., p. 53.
9. Ibid., p. 83.
10. Ibid., p. 127.
11. Ibid., p. 184.
12. Jean-Paul Sartre, *Being and Nothingness*, Translated by Hazel E. Barnes (Washington Square Pros, U.S.A., 1956) p. 29.
13. Jean-Paul Sartre, *Nausea*, p. 22.
14. Ibid., p. 35.
15. Ibid., p. 143.
16. Jean-Paul Sartre, *The Psychology of Imagination*, Translated by Bernard Frechtman (Philosophical Library, New York, 1948) p. 272.
17. Jean-Paul Sartre, *The Emotions: Outline of a Theory*,

Translated by Bernard Frechtman (Philosophical Library, New York), p. 57.

18. Jean-Paul Sartre, *Being and Nothingness*, p. 5.
19. Ibid., p. 5.
20. Ibid., p. 8.
21. Jean-Paul Sartre, *Nausea*, p. 143.
22. Ibid., pp. 192-193.
23. Jean-Paul Sartre, *Being and Nothingness*, p. 11.
24. Jean-Paul Sartre, *The Transcendence of the Ego*, p. 40.
25. Jean-Paul Sartre, *Being and Nothingness*, p. 12.
26. Ibid., p. 239.
27. Ibid., pp. 12-13.
28. Jean-Paul Sartre,*The Transcendence of the Ego*, pp. 44-49.
29. Ibid., p. 106.
30. Jean-Paul Sartre, *Being and Nothingness*, p. 16.
31. Ibid., p. 17.
32. Jean-Paul Sartre, *Nausea*, p. 145.
33. Jean-Paul Sartre, *Being and Nothingness*, p. 21.
34. Ibid., p. 24.
35. Ibid., p. 24.
36. Ibid., p. 24.
37. Jean-Paul Sartre, *Nausea*, p. 181.
38. Ibid., p. 190.
39. Ibid., p. 189.
40. Jean-Paul Sartre, *Being and Nothingness*, pp. 26-27.
41. Ibid., p. 28.
42. Ibid., p. 29.
43. Ibid., p. 29.
44. Ibid., p. 29.
45. Jean-Paul Sartre, *Nausea*, pp. 184-185.
46. Jean-Paul Sartre, *Being and Nothingness*, p. 38.
47. Ibid., p. 39.
48. Ibid., p. 42.
49. Ibid., p. 43.

50. Ibid., p. 47.
51. Ibid., pp. 48-49.
52. Ibid., p. 57.
53. Ibid., p. 57.
54. Ibid., p. 59.
55. Ibid., p. 60.
56. Ibid., p. 65.
57. Ibid., p. 67.
58. Ibid., p. 68.
59. Ibid., pp. 76-77.
60. Ibid., p. 121.
61. Ibid., p. 122.
62. Ibid., p. 125.
63. Ibid., p. 126.
64. Ibid., p. 800.
65. Ibid., pp. 78-79.
66. Ibid., p. 83.
67. Ibid., p. 83.
68. Ibid., p. 86.
69. Ibid., p. 88.
70. Ibid., p. 89.
71. Ibid., p. 90.
72. Ibid., p. 98.
73. Ibid., p. 101.
74. Ibid., p. 102.
75. Ibid., p. 112.
76. Ibid., p. 115.
77. Ibid., p. 116.
78. Ibid., p. 127.
79. Ibid., p. 127.
80. Jean-Paul Sartre, *Nausea*, p. 188.
81. Supra No. 20, *Being and Nothingness*, p. 128.
82. Ibid., p. 128.
83. Ibid., p. 129.
84. Ibid., p. 130.
85. Ibid., p. 131.

86. Ibid., p. 132.
87. Ibid., p. 134.
88. Ibid., p. 134.
89. Ibid., p. 135.
90. Ibid., p. 136.
91. Ibid., p. 137.
92. Ibid., p. 139.
93. Ibid., p. 140.
94. Ibid., p. 152.
95. Ibid., p. 155.
96. Ibid., p. 156.
97. Ibid., p. 159.
98. Ibid., p. 163.
99. Ibid., p. 172.
100. Ibid., p. 173.
101. Ibid., p. 177.
102. Ibid., p. 179.
103. Ibid., p. 181.
104. Ibid., p. 185.
105. Ibid., p. 202.
106. Ibid., p. 188.
107. Ibid., p. 198.
108. Ibid., p. 202.
109. Ibid., p. 203.
110. Ibid., p. 239.
111. Ibid., p. 301.
112. Ibid., p. 302.
113. Ibid., p. 313.
114. Ibid., p. 340.
115. Ibid., p. 343.
116. Ibid., p. 345.
117. Ibid., p. 348.
118. Ibid., p. 352.
119. Ibid., pp. 381-382.
120. Ibid., p. 390.
121. Ibid., p. 400.

122. Ibid., p. 402.
123. Ibid., pp. 407-408.
124. Ibid., pp. 411-412.
125. Ibid., p. 428.
126. Ibid., p. 432.
127. Ibid., p. 445.
128. Ibid., p. 445.
129. Ibid., p. 448.
130. Ibid., p. 452.
131. Ibid., p. 457.
132. Ibid., p. 460.
133. Ibid., p. 462.
134. Ibid., p. 472.
135. Ibid., p. 473.
136. Ibid., p. 474.
137. Ibid., p. 477.
138. Ibid., p. 491.
139. Ibid., p. 503.
140. Ibid., pp. 509-510.
141. Ibid., p. 523.
142. Ibid., p. 529.
143. Ibid., p. 532.
144. Ibid., p. 533.
145. Ibid., p. 535.
146. Ibid., p. 541.
147. Ibid., p. 542.
148. Ibid., p. 544.
149. Ibid., p. 549.
150. Ibid., p. 555.
151. Jean-Paul Sartre, *Existentialism and Humanism*, Translated by Philip Mairet (Methuen & Co. Ltd, Great Britain, 1948), p. 37.
152. Jean-Paul Sartre, *Being and Nothingness*, p. 560.
153. Ibid., p. 564.
154. Ibid., p. 567.
155. Ibid., pp. 568-569.

156. Ibid., pp. 593-594.
157. Ibid., p. 597.
158. Ibid., p. 607.
159. Ibid., p. 619.
160. Ibid., p. 626.
161. Ibid., p. 628.
162. Ibid., p. 629.
163. Ibid., p. 629.
164. Ibid., p. 634.
165. Ibid., p. 638.
166. Ibid., p. 640.
167. Ibid., p. 647.
168. Ibid., p. 654.
169. Ibid., p. 657.
170. Ibid., p. 685.
171. Ibid., p. 687.
172. Ibid., p. 694.
173. Ibid., p. 698.
174. Ibid., pp. 707-708.
175. Ibid., p. 710.
176. Ibid., p. 32.
177. Ibid., p. 724.
178. Ibid., p. 731.
179. Ibid., p. 734.
180. Ibid., p. 736.
181. Ibid., p. 747.
182. Ibid., p. 757.
183. Ibid., p. 764.
184. Ibid., p. 784.
185. Ibid., p. 788.
186. Ibid., p. 788.
187. Ibid., p. 796.
188. Ibid., p. 798.
189. Jean-Paul Sartre, *Existentialism and Humanism*, p. 29.
190. Ibid., p. 30.

191. Ibid., p. 38.
192. Ibid., p. 67.
193. Robert Denoon Cumming, *The Philosophy of Jean-Paul Sartre,* (Vintage Books, U.K.,1965), p. 38.
194. Jean-Paul Sartre, *Search for a Method,* Translated by Hazel E. Barnes (Knopf, New York, 1963), pp. 151-152.
195. Robert Denoon Cumming, *The Philosophy of Jean-Paul Sartre,* p. 41.
196. Jean-Paul Sartre, *The Critique of Dialectical Reason,* Translated by Hazel E. Barnes (Knopf, New York, 1963), p. 456.
197. Jean-Paul Sartre, *Search for a Method,* p. 158.
198. Jean-Paul Sartre, *The Critique of Dialectical Reason,* p. 45.
199. Ibid., p. 50.
200. Ibid., p. 79.
201. Ibid., p. 80.
202. Ibid., p. 81.
203. Ibid., p. 91.
204. Ibid., p. 100.
205. Ibid., p. 100.
206. Ibid., p. 103.
207. Ibid., p. 109.
208. Ibid., p. 110.
209. Ibid., p. 126.
210. Ibid., p. 126.
211. Ibid., p. 127.
212. Ibid., p. 128.
213. Ibid., p. 129.
214. Ibid., p. 130.
215. Ibid., pp. 131-132.
216. Ibid., p. 132.
217. Ibid., p. 136.
218. Ibid., p. 137.
219. Ibid., p. 154.

220. Ibid., p. 180.
221. Ibid., pp. 180-181.
222a. Ibid., p. 221.
222b. Ibid., p. 224.
223. Ibid., p. 230.
224. Ibid., p. 235.
225. Ibid., pp. 256-257.
226. Ibid., p. 260.
227. Ibid., p. 261.
228. Ibid., p. 271.
229. Ibid., p. 325.
230. Ibid., p. 349.
231. Ibid., p. 386.
232. Ibid., p. 583.
233. Ibid., p. 583.
234. Jean-Paul Sartre, *Being and Nothingness*, p. 784.
235. Kaufmann, *Existentialism*, p. 46.
236. Jean-Paul Sartre, *Existentialism and Humanism*, p. 35.
237. Ibid., p. 53.
238. Ibid., p. 31.
239. Ibid., p. 55.
240. Ibid., p. 66.

Bibliography

Works by Jean Paul Sartre

1. *The Transcendence of the Ego* (1936), translated by Forest Williams and Robert Kirkpatrick (Noonday, New York, 1957).
2. *Nausea* (1938), translated by Robert Baldick (Penguin Books Ltd., London, 1963).
3. *The Emotions: Outline of a Theory* (1939), translated by Bernard Frechtman (Philosophical Library, New York, 1939).
4. *The Psychology of Imagination* (1940), translated by Bernard Frechtman (Philosophical Library, New York, 1948).
5. *Being and Nothingness* (1943), translated by Hazel E. Barnes (Washington Square Pros, U.S.A., 1956).
6. *Existentialism and Humanism*, translated by Philip Mairet (Methuen & Co. Ltd, Great Britain, 1948).
7. *Search for a Method* (1957), translated by Hazel E. Barnes (Knopf, New York, 1963).
8. *The Critique of Dialectical Reason* (1960), translated by Hazel E. Barnes (Knopf, New York, 1963).
9. *The Words – The Autobiography of Jean-Paul Sartre* (1964), translated by Bernard Frechtman (Vintage Books, New York, 1964).

Secondary Works

1. Arbaugh E. George and Arbaugh B. George, *Kierkegaard's Authorship*, (George Allen & Unwin Ltd., London, 1968).

2. Blackham, H.J., *Existential Thinkers*, (Lowe & Brydone, London, 1961).

3. Cumming Denoon Robert, *The Philosophy of Jean-Paul Sartre*, (Vintage Books, New York, 1965).

4. Roubiczec Paul, *Existentialism For and Against*, (Cambridge University Press, U.K., 1964).

5. Taylor C. Mark, *Kierkegaard's Pseudonymous Authorship*, (Princeton University Press, Princeton, 1973).

6. *The Cambridge Companion to Kierkegaard*, (Cambridge University Press, U.K., 1998).

Index